RTB:

Return To Being

RTB:
Return To Being

A Veteran's Journey
Through Identity, Purpose,
and Transition

Rick Padilla

BLACKSMITH PUBLISHING 2013

Return to Being: A Veteran's Journey Through Identity, Purpose, and Transition

ISBN 978-1956-9-04499

Printed in the United States of America

Published by Blacksmith LLC
Fayetteville, North Carolina

www.BlacksmithPublishing.com

Direct inquiries and/or orders to the above web address.

Dedication

To Ash, Harper, Eli, and Maddox—
Thank you for saving my life. For giving me a reason to find my way back.
Without you, my life is incomplete. I love you—ten times, 95, to the moon and back...until the sun comes back.
To the fallen brothers and sisters, we have lost—those who couldn't find a way to feel like they still belonged—we will not forget you.
To the families of the fallen, there are no words that can fully capture the loss you have endured. My hope with this is simple—that no other family has to carry that same pain.
And to those who are still in it... who feel like there isn't a way out—
There is.
And I will walk that path with you. You are not alone.
And you matter—more than you may ever realize.

Before You Begin

This isn't a book about having it all figured out. It's not a guide written by someone who got everything right, or someone who found a perfect way through. It's written by someone who didn't. Someone who lost direction. Someone who tried to force his way through things that couldn't be forced. Someone who kept moving long after it stopped making sense, because stopping didn't feel like an option.

There are parts of this story that aren't clean. Parts that don't resolve neatly. Parts that took longer to understand than I expected, and longer to fix than I want to admit. I'm not writing this from a place of perfection. I'm writing from a place of having gone through it... I'm still going through it.

Because transition doesn't end the day you leave. It doesn't end when you get a job. It doesn't end when things start to look stable on the outside. For a lot of us, it's quieter than that. It shows up in the moments no one sees, in the space between who you were and who you're supposed to be now, and in the questions you don't always know how to ask out loud.

Who am I without this? What am I supposed to do now? Why doesn't this feel the way I thought it would?

If you've asked yourself any of those questions, you're not alone.

That's what this book is really about. Not answers. Not a perfect path. Awareness. Understanding what might actually be happening beneath the surface, so you're not walking through it thinking something is wrong with you.

Because for a long time, that's what I believed. I thought I lacked discipline. I thought I had lost something I couldn't get back. I thought I was the problem.

It took time, and a lot of uncomfortable honesty, to realize something different. I wasn't broken. I just didn't understand what I was going through. And when you don't understand something, it's easy to turn it inward. To assume it's personal failure instead of a process. This book is my way of laying that process out—not as a blueprint, but as a lived experience.

You'll see what it looked like for me, unfiltered. The moments I got it wrong. The habits that made things worse. The points where I knew better and still didn't do better. And eventually, the moments when something started to shift. Not all at once. Not in a clean line. Just enough to change direction.

As you read this, you don't need to have everything figured out. You don't need to relate to every part of my story. You don't need to agree with everything I say.

All I ask is this: Be honest with yourself.

If something in here feels familiar, don't brush it off. If something makes you uncomfortable, sit with it for a minute. If something feels like it hits a little too close to home, that might be worth paying attention to.

You don't have to rush through this. There's no finish line waiting at the end of these pages. This isn't about getting somewhere. It's about understanding where you are, and why it feels the way it does.

Because once you can see it clearly, you can't start to move forward differently. Not perfectly. Not all at once. But intentionally.

Return to being doesn't happen in a single moment. It happens in small shifts, in awareness, and in the decision to stop pretending something is okay when it isn't.

And if you're here—if you picked this up, if you're even willing to look at this part of your life—you've already taken a step most people avoid.

That matters. More than you probably realize. Take your time with this. There's nothing you need to prove here. Just read. And be honest.

That's enough.

Return to Being

Contents

1

When the Mission Ends

The Moment It Started

My transition didn't begin the day I left the Army. It didn't start with paperwork, a briefing, or a final formation. It started long before anyone told me it was over. It started in Afghanistan.

It was 2019, about halfway through a nine-month deployment. At the time, nothing about it felt unusual—at least not on the surface. We were in direct support of an ODA out of 10th Group, and our MEDEVAC company was running at a tempo higher than anyone had expected. Missions were happening almost every night. Aircraft were split across multiple sites, which meant crews were constantly rotating, constantly moving, and rarely in the same place long enough to reset. Crews were stretched thin, and leadership was spread across distance, darkness, and constant demand. It wasn't the kind of pressure you talked about. It was the kind you just stepped into and carried without question.

Everyone felt it. But responsibility doesn't distribute evenly.

Looking back now, that's the part I understand differently. At the time, it didn't feel like I was taking on more than I should. It felt like I was doing exactly what I was supposed to do. There wasn't a moment where I stopped and questioned whether the pace was sustainable or whether the weight I was carrying was too much. There was just an unspoken expectation—one I had internalized long before that deployment—that if something needed to be handled, I would handle it.

Somewhere along the way, I made a decision—one that felt right at the time, and honestly, one I still stand by. If something was going to land hard, it was going to land on me first. Not because I wanted recognition, and not because I had something to prove. It was simpler than that. That's what I believed leadership was. You don't let your people get crushed. You absorb what you can. You carry what others don't have to.

So I stepped into it.

Not just when it was convenient. Not just when it was expected. Every problem. Every shortfall. Every decision that carried weight—I took it. If something went wrong, I stepped forward before it could fall on someone else. If something was missing, I filled the gap. If something felt like it was about to break, I put myself in the place where it would break first.

And for a while, it worked. At least, it looked like it did.

From the outside, I was still functioning. Still leading. Still showing up the way I was supposed to. I was making decisions, running missions, managing people, and keeping everything moving forward. No one saw anything breaking, because I didn't let them. There wasn't space for that, and even if there had been, I wouldn't have used it. That wasn't how I operated.

What I didn't understand at the time was that just because something looks sustainable doesn't mean it is. You can carry weight for a long time and convince yourself it's manageable, especially when nothing around you is visibly falling apart. But that doesn't mean the cost isn't building somewhere you can't see yet.

Pressure doesn't disappear just because you carry it well. It accumulates quietly. The dangerous part is you don't feel it all at once. It builds in the background, layer by layer, so gradually that you convince yourself you're fine... right up until the moment you're not.

And eventually, whether you're ready or not, your body decides it's had enough.

The First Break

The first time it happened, I didn't have a name for it. I just knew something was wrong. It started subtle. My chest tightened—not sharp, just enough to notice. I remember thinking, *that's weird.* It wasn't pain. Not yet. Just pressure, like something was sitting on my chest. Light at first, but enough that I couldn't ignore it. It didn't feel urgent, just out of place, like something small had shifted and I couldn't quite figure out why.

For a second, I tried to write it off. Like maybe I was just tired. Maybe I hadn't eaten. Maybe it was nothing. That's what made the most sense in the moment—to reduce it, to make it smaller than it felt. So I did what I had always done. I pushed through it.

I kept moving. Kept talking. Kept acting like nothing was off, because people were around me—and the last thing I was going to do was let them see me lose control. That wasn't an option. Not in that environment. Not in that role. You don't stop. You don't step away. You definitely don't become the problem. But it didn't stop.

The pressure didn't spread outward—it moved inward. Tightening. Closing. Like something inside my chest was slowly locking up. At first, I tried to ignore it, to treat it like something temporary that would pass if I just stayed focused on what I was doing. But the more I tried to push past it, the more it demanded my attention. I tried to take a breath. That's when it hit me. Something wasn't right.

It didn't feel like breathing anymore. It felt like I was trying to remember how to do something my body should have known automatically—like the connection between my mind and my lungs had been cut. I pulled in air, but it didn't feel like enough. So I tried again. Deeper this time. Still nothing. And that's when everything else started to fade.

Not all at once. Just enough that I noticed it. Conversations around me blurred. The noise in the room dropped off, like someone had turned the volume down just slightly. My focus narrowed without me choosing it to. Everything that wasn't happening inside my chest stopped mattering.

That's when my attention locked onto it. Fully. No more pretending. No more ignoring. Everything else faded into the background, and all that was left was what was happening inside my chest. Something was wrong. Bad wrong.

I stepped out of the Battalion TOC. I don't remember making the decision—I just knew I couldn't stay there. Not like that. Not where people could see me. There was a level of exposure in that space that I couldn't risk. If something was happening, I needed it to happen somewhere else. Somewhere contained. Even that thought didn't fully make sense—but it was automatic. Get out. Contain it. Don't let anyone see.

Every step back to the platoon area felt off, like I wasn't fully in control of my body anymore. My movements didn't feel as automatic as they should have. My awareness narrowed, not by choice, but because it had to. My heart was racing, but not in a way I recognized.

Not adrenaline. Not controlled. Erratic. Unpredictable. There's a difference between a body responding to a threat and a body that feels like it's turning on itself. I had experienced the first one plenty of times. This wasn't that. There was no external cause, nothing to react to, nothing to fix. Just internal chaos. And that's what made it worse. Because there was nothing to fight.

My breathing got worse—short, fast, shallow. I found my PSG and forced the words out. "I don't feel right. I can't catch my breath." Even saying it felt wrong, like I was crossing a line I wasn't supposed to cross. Leaders don't say things like that. Leaders don't admit that something is off.

But I didn't have a choice. They didn't hesitate. They laid me down on the couch. I remember the fabric against my back—the way it felt too soft for what was happening, like I didn't belong there. The room didn't match the moment. It felt disconnected, like everything around me was normal, and I was the only thing that wasn't.

Someone grabbed my wrist, checking my pulse. Another watched my chest, counting, tracking, assessing. I could feel all of it—the contact, the movement, the presence of people trying to figure out what was happening.

And none of it made me feel better. Because inside my head... everything was getting worse. The thought hit fast.

I'm having a heart attack.

Not a question. Not a guess. A fact. At least, that's what it felt like. There was no space for doubt in that moment. Everything I was experiencing lined up with one conclusion, and once that thought took hold, it took over everything else.

My world narrowed. Sound dropped off. Voices blurred together, like they were there but far away. My vision tunneled—the edges fading, the center locking in. Time didn't stop, but it slowed just enough for one realization to settle in, clear and unavoidable. This is it. I'm going to die right here. And then another thought came right behind it. *And I can't stop it.* That was the part that broke something. Because control was the one thing I had always relied on. Training, experience, repetition—everything we did was built around control. Control the situation. Control yourself. Control the outcome. And in that moment... I had none of it.

No amount of effort. No amount of focus. Nothing I was trying was working. I couldn't breathe the way I needed to breathe. I couldn't slow my heart down. I couldn't think my way out of it.

And that scared me more than anything else. Then someone said it. "You're having a panic attack." That didn't make sense. Because in my head, this wasn't panic. This was real. This was physical. This was my body failing. And now they were telling me it wasn't? That it was something else? Something in my head? I didn't know what to do with that. Confusion hit first. Then something else came right behind it. Embarrassment.

I was a leader—the one people looked to when things went wrong. The one who was supposed to be steady, controlled, reliable. The one who handled situations like this, not the one laying in the middle of one. And I was laying there. Unable to breathe. Unable to control my own body. Having a panic attack. I remember thinking, *what the hell is wrong with me?* And that question hit harder than anything physical that was happening in that moment. Because it wasn't just about what I was feeling—it was about what it meant. If this was happening to me, if I couldn't control something this basic, then what else could I not control?

Even as it started to pass—even as my breathing slowly came back and my body started to settle—that question didn't go away. It didn't resolve. It didn't fade. It just... stayed. Sitting there in the background. Unanswered. I couldn't explain it. I couldn't control it. And I had no idea if it was going to happen again. I Thought I had It Back

After that first episode, I was able to talk to someone, and for the first time, things started to make a little more sense. Not all of it—but enough to where I didn't feel completely lost inside my own head anymore. It didn't give me a full explanation, and it didn't erase what had happened, but it gave me something I didn't have before.

Context. It gave me a way to frame it, to put boundaries around something that had felt completely out of control. And sometimes, that's all you need to start moving forward again. Not answers—just something that makes it feel like you're not dealing with something random or unexplainable.

It gave me something to hold onto, something that made it feel like what I had experienced wasn't completely out of nowhere.

More than anything, though, my leadership still trusted me. They trusted me to lead, to fly, to stay in the fight and be part of the team. That mattered more than I realized at the time. It wasn't just about the job—it was about what that trust represented. It meant I was still valued, still needed, still seen as someone who could carry their weight.

And that did something for me internally. Because if they still saw me that way, then maybe nothing had really changed. Maybe that moment on the couch didn't define anything. Maybe it was just an isolated incident. It felt like proof that I was still who I thought I was.

The therapist helped more than I expected. She didn't try to force anything or push me into some version of progress I wasn't ready for. She met me where I was, which mattered more than anything else. There wasn't pressure to fix it immediately or to turn it into something bigger than I was ready to face. Instead, she gave me tools—simple things, but things that worked. Ways to slow everything down when it started to build. Ways to create space between what I was feeling and how I reacted to it. Ways to regain a sense of control when it felt like it was slipping. And for a while, it felt like those tools were enough. Not perfect. Not permanent. But enough.

I settled back into the routine. Back into the mission. Back into the role I understood. I started flying again, running missions, getting back into a rhythm that had always made things feel clear and predictable. There was something about being back in that environment that made everything else quiet down. Out there, things still made sense.

Even when we were taking fire, even when things got chaotic, there was structure in it. There was a problem, there was a response, and there was a role to play. Everything had a place, and everything had a purpose. There was no room for overthinking, no space for internal noise. No confusion. No hesitation. No second-guessing. Just action.

Just movement. Just doing what I had been trained to do. And strangely enough, that felt normal. It felt controlled.

It felt like I had found my footing again, like I had stepped back into something stable after slipping for a moment. The contrast between that first episode and being back in the aircraft, back in the mission, made it easy to believe that whatever had happened wasn't something that would define me moving forward.

In a way, it almost felt like a reward—like I had pushed through something and earned my way back to where I was supposed to be. Like I had proven, at least to myself, that I still had it. That whatever had happened before wasn't the beginning of something bigger.

That it didn't mean anything. And that belief was quiet, but it was strong. It sat underneath everything I was doing, reinforcing the idea that I was fine, that I was still capable, that I hadn't lost anything that mattered.

Like maybe—just maybe—everything was going to be okay.

The Weight I Was Carrying

At the time, I didn't connect that moment to anything bigger. I treated it like an isolated event—something that happened, something I could work through, and then move past. It didn't feel like a warning sign or the beginning of anything. It just felt like something I needed to get under control, something that didn't fit and needed to be corrected so I could get back to operating the way I always had. I wasn't looking for meaning. I was looking for control. But it wasn't an isolated event.

I wasn't just operating in one role over there. I was constantly moving back and forth between being a Battle Captain and a Section Leader, trying to function at two different levels at the same time. One minute I was managing the fight—tracking missions, coordinating aircraft, making sure crews were where they needed to be, thinking at a higher level about how everything fit together. The next, I was responsible for my people directly, making sure they were covered, taken care of, and not getting crushed by everything coming down from above. It wasn't just a shift in responsibility. It was a constant shift in mindset.

And there was no pause between the two. No moment to reset, no space to transition cleanly from one role to the other. It was immediate, continuous, and expected. One demand flowed straight into the next, and over time, that kind of constant switching starts to wear on you in ways that aren't obvious while you're in it. Because you're still functioning. You're still getting it done. So you assume you're fine.

The tempo we were running at only made that harder. On paper, we were operating as a battalion-minus element, but in reality, it required more than we had—more aircraft, more personnel, more depth than we could actually sustain over time. There was a gap between what was required and what was available, and that gap didn't get addressed.

The unit that replaced us eventually brought that capability. We didn't. So the gap didn't go away. It didn't get fixed. It got absorbed. And like everything else, that absorption didn't spread evenly. It rolled downhill. Stress always does. The weight of what wasn't there—the missing people, the missing capacity, the expectations that didn't change—had to land somewhere. It had to settle somewhere in order for the system to keep functioning. It landed on me. Because I made sure it did.

Somewhere in all of that, I made another decision. One that, again, felt right at the time. I wasn't going to let that pressure hit my people. Not if I could take it instead. That wasn't something I thought through in a strategic way—it was automatic. It was built into how I understood leadership. So I absorbed it.

Every missed expectation, every shortfall, every frustration coming from higher—I took it. I took the blame before it reached them. I took the pressure before it had a chance to spread. I took the hits so they didn't have to. I positioned myself between them and everything coming down, acting as a buffer so they could focus on what they needed to do without carrying the full weight of everything behind it.

Because that's what I believed a leader was supposed to do.

Protect your people, even if it costs you.

At the time, I didn't question that belief. I didn't consider whether there were limits to it or whether there was a point where absorbing more would stop being effective and start becoming damaging. It just felt right, and in that environment, feeling right was enough.

What I didn't understand then was that there is always a cost.

It doesn't show up all at once, and it doesn't make itself obvious. It builds quietly, underneath everything else, in ways you don't notice while you're in it. There's no clear moment where you feel it stacking in real time. You just keep going, keep carrying, keep telling yourself you've got it, because nothing around you is visibly breaking.

Until something does. And when it finally surfaces, it doesn't ask for permission. That night on the couch—that wasn't just a panic attack. It was everything I had been holding finally pushing back. Every piece of pressure I thought I had managed, every weight I thought I had absorbed—it all showed up at once. Not gradually, not in a way I could track or understand in the moment, but all at once, overwhelming and undeniable. And I didn't recognize it for what it was. I didn't see it as a signal. I didn't see it as something that needed to be understood or addressed in a different way.

And right behind it, something else started to take hold. Not understanding. Not awareness. Embarrassment. Then shame. Because I didn't see it as a signal. I saw it as failure.

The Second Break

I wish I could say I slowed down after that—that I recognized something was wrong and made an adjustment. I didn't. If anything, I doubled down. Because now it wasn't just pressure anymore. There was something else mixed into it—something I didn't fully understand, but I knew it didn't belong. I had seen a crack, and instead of dealing with it, I tried to cover it up. I told myself the answer was to push harder, move faster, and make sure it didn't happen again. That became the goal. Not understanding it. Not addressing it. Preventing it.

And for a while, I convinced myself it was working. On the surface, nothing looked off. I was still doing what I had always done, still operating the way I was expected to. I was showing up, making decisions, leading, executing. There were no obvious signs to anyone else that something had shifted. And because of that, I told myself nothing had. If I could still perform, then I was fine. If no one else saw it, then it didn't matter. Until the day it didn't.

It was a no-notice evaluation—nothing outside the scope of what I had done before. Under normal conditions, it wouldn't have mattered. It was routine, something I knew how to handle without thinking. It was the kind of thing I had done enough times that it should have been automatic. But these weren't normal conditions anymore.

Even if I was still trying to treat them like they were. Everything felt different. Not externally—nothing about the environment had changed. The task was the same. The expectations were the same. The standard was the same. But internally, everything had shifted.

There was a kind of noise that hadn't been there before. Not loud, not obvious—but constant. Every thought carried weight. Every movement felt amplified. Things that used to happen automatically now felt deliberate, like I had to think through each step instead of just executing it. There was no separation between what I needed to focus on and everything else running through my head.

It all blended together. And the more I tried to organize it, the worse it got. The harder I tried to lock in, the less control I felt like I had. My attention didn't narrow—it scattered. Instead of focusing on what mattered, I became aware of everything at once, and none of it felt manageable. That was new. That was something I didn't know how to operate through. And then it hit. Not confusion. Not hesitation. Collapse.

There was no gradual build this time, no moment where I could feel it coming and try to get ahead of it. It wasn't something I could push through or contain until later. It happened right there, in the moment, in front of everything I had been trying to hold together.

There was no space to recover. No way to redirect it. No fallback. Just a complete loss of control in a place where I had always relied on having it. And that's what made it different from the first time. The first time, I was alone enough to step away. This time, I wasn't. This time, it was visible. And that changed everything.

Because it wasn't just something I experienced internally anymore—it was something that existed in the same space as everyone else. Even if they didn't fully understand it, even if they didn't see all of it, I knew it had crossed that line. I couldn't contain it anymore. And just like that, one thought cut through everything else and took over. I'm failing. Not just in that moment. Not just in that evaluation. Everywhere.

It wasn't a logical conclusion. It wasn't something I worked through step by step. It was immediate and absolute. One moment of loss of control turned into a judgment about everything—my ability to lead, my ability to perform, my ability to be who I thought I was supposed to be. And once that thought took hold, it didn't stay contained to that moment. It spread.

Because if I couldn't control myself here, in something I had done a hundred times before... Then what else couldn't I control?

The Moment It Became Real

Not long after that, they made the call. They grounded me, took my weapon, and pulled me out of a role I had built my entire identity around. I remember sitting there, hearing it—understanding exactly what was being said, while at the same time not fully accepting it. The words registered, but they didn't land the way they should have.

It didn't feel like something that was actually happening to me. It felt distant. Disconnected. Like I was watching it unfold instead of being in it. There was a strange separation between what I was hearing and what I was feeling. Logically, I knew what it meant. I understood the implications. I knew what being grounded represented, what it said about where I stood, and what it would likely lead to. But emotionally, it hadn't caught up yet. And maybe that was a form of protection.

Because if it had all landed at once—if I had fully processed what was happening in that moment—I don't know that I would have been able to sit there the way I did. I don't know that I would have been able to hold it together. So instead, it stayed at a distance. Something I could observe. Something I could acknowledge. But not something I fully let in.

Because officially, nothing had ended yet. I was still there. Still in uniform. Still part of the unit. On paper, everything looked the same, and from the outside, there was no clear moment that marked an ending. There was no ceremony, no announcement, no defined line that separated "before" from "after."

Everything still looked intact. And that made it easier to pretend that it was. But internally, something had already shifted. It wasn't loud or dramatic. There wasn't a single defining moment where everything stopped. It didn't feel like something breaking in real time. It was quieter than that—more of a realization settling in than something hitting all at once.

A slow recognition. A quiet understanding that didn't need to be said out loud to be real. Even if no one had said it directly, even if nothing had been finalized or processed yet, I knew. Something in me had already made the connection. Not based on what someone told me, but based on what I had felt, what I had experienced, and what I could no longer ignore. My time in the Army—at least the version of it I understood—was over. And that realization didn't come with clarity. It came with absence.

There was no immediate sense of what came next, no direction to shift toward, no structure to replace what I was losing. The role I had built myself around, the identity I had operated within, the expectations I had always known how to meet—all of it was tied to something that no longer felt accessible. And I didn't know what to do with that.

There was no transition plan for that kind of realization. No checklist. No briefing. No step-by-step process to follow that could help make sense of what it meant or how to move forward from it.

So I defaulted to what I had always done. I kept showing up. I stayed in the routine, stayed in the structure, acted like nothing had changed because I didn't know how to do anything else. There was comfort in that, even if it wasn't real comfort. It was familiar. It was something I could hold onto while everything else felt uncertain. From the outside, it probably looked the same. Like I was still there. Still functioning. Still part of the system. But underneath that, everything had already changed. The role was still there. The structure was still there. But the connection to it wasn't. And that's what made it real.

The Flight Back

I wasn't afraid when I was getting shot at. That's the part that still stands out to me. When things were kinetic—when rounds were coming in, when everything moved fast and decisions had to be made immediately—there was no hesitation, no second-guessing, no internal debate. My body knew exactly what to do.

Training took over, muscle memory carried it, and there was no space for fear. There was only action. Moving. Reacting. Executing. That's where I was supposed to be. That's where everything made sense. There was clarity in that environment, even in the middle of chaos. You didn't have time to think about yourself. You didn't have time to question anything. You just did what needed to be done, and that was enough.

But sitting on that flight back to Bagram was different. There was no chaos. No urgency. No mission pulling my focus forward. No immediate problem to solve, no task that demanded my full attention. Just time. Time to sit. Time to think. Time to feel everything I had been outrunning up to that point. And that's when the fear showed up. Not the kind I expected. Not fear of dying. Something else entirely. Fear of being seen.

I remember sitting there, staring straight ahead, trying to keep my breathing steady and my posture normal, making sure no one around me noticed anything was off. Because now I knew it could happen again, and I didn't know when, or why, or how to stop it. That uncertainty sat in the background of everything, quietly shaping how I moved, how I breathed, and how I carried myself. Every small shift in my body pulled my attention—every breath, every heartbeat, every slight change in how I felt. Things that should have been automatic became something I monitored constantly. I wasn't just sitting there—I was tracking myself, watching for signs, waiting for something to go wrong. Bracing for it. Trying to stay ahead of something I didn't fully understand. And the more I paid attention to it, the more it felt like I was losing control over it.

That was the part I couldn't shake. Because control had always been the constant, and now it wasn't. Underneath all of that, there was another thought I couldn't ignore. I knew I was going to have to face my commander. Not because I thought I was in trouble, and not because I expected him to react negatively, but because I didn't know how he would see me now. Before all of this, I knew exactly who I was in that unit. I knew my role. I knew what I brought to the table. I knew how I fit into the bigger picture. There was no question about where I stood or how I was viewed. Now, I didn't. And that uncertainty sat heavier than anything else. It wasn't just about what had happened. It was about what it meant.

I started replaying everything—the panic attack, the evaluation, every moment I thought I had come up short—over and over again. Not casually, not in passing, but deliberately, like I was searching for something. Searching for proof that something had changed, that I wasn't who I was supposed to be anymore. And the more I replayed it, the more convinced I became that it had. I started believing I was slipping, that I wasn't reliable anymore, that I wasn't what my leadership expected. Once that belief started to settle in, everything else began to align with it. Every small doubt reinforced it. Every moment of hesitation confirmed it. It didn't matter what was actually happening around me—internally, I had already started rewriting who I was.

By the time we landed, I had already decided what he was going to see. Not a leader. Not someone dependable. Someone broken. Someone who couldn't handle it anymore. But when I finally stood in front of him, that's not what I got. He didn't pull away. He didn't treat me differently. He didn't look at me like I was done or like something had been taken from me. He made time for me, talked to me like nothing had changed, like I still belonged there and still had a place in the company. Like I was still me.

Then he told me something I didn't expect—that he wanted me to stay on as a platoon leader when we got back. He still trusted me. Still had confidence in me. Still saw value in me. I remember standing there hearing it and not knowing what to do with it, because it didn't match what I believed about myself. Not even close. On one side, I had someone I respected—someone who knew the job and the standard—looking at me like I was still capable. On the other side, I had my own voice, and that voice was louder. Relentless. Pointing out every mistake, every moment of doubt, every sign that I wasn't holding it together the way I should. And no matter what he said, that voice didn't get quieter. It got stronger.

So I stood there, nodding, acknowledging what he was saying, but not believing a word of it. Not because I didn't trust him, but because internally I had already made a different call. And that's the part that's hard to explain. When everyone around you shows you respect, confidence, and support, and you can't feel any of it, it creates a kind of isolation that doesn't make sense from the outside. You're surrounded by people who believe in you, and you still feel completely alone, because no one else can hear what's going on in your head or feel the weight of it the way you do.

That disconnect is where things really start to break. Because externally, nothing had changed. I was still in a combat zone, still wearing the uniform, still surrounded by my people. Everything around me was intact. The system was still there. The expectations were still there. But internally, everything had shifted. In my own mind, I wasn't effective anymore. I saw myself as a liability, and I hated myself for it—for what I believed was weakness, for not being able to push through it the way I always had before. And the harder I was on myself, the quieter I became about it, because the last thing I was going to do was let anyone else see it.

Functioning While Falling Apart

After that conversation, nothing really changed—at least not on the surface. I still showed up, still wore the uniform, still did everything I was supposed to do. If you looked at me from the outside, you wouldn't have seen anything different. I wasn't missing formations, I wasn't causing problems, and I wasn't breaking down in front of anyone. I was still there in every way that mattered to everyone else, and that was part of the problem. As long as everything looked the same, there was no reason for anyone to think anything had changed. But something had. It just wasn't visible.

It was something I felt constantly, something that sat in the background of everything I did. It wasn't loud enough to stop me, but it was persistent enough that I couldn't ignore it no matter how hard I tried to push it down. It followed me into every interaction, every decision, every moment where I had to engage with the role I was still expected to fill. Every interaction started to feel different—not because people treated me differently, but because I was second-guessing everything. The way I spoke, the way I responded, even the way I existed in conversations. Things that used to feel automatic suddenly felt deliberate, almost forced, like I was thinking through actions that had once happened naturally without effort.

That shift is hard to explain if you haven't experienced it. It's not that you forget how to do what you've always done. It's that you stop trusting yourself to do it the same way. Once that trust is gone, everything slows down. Everything becomes something you have to think through instead of something you can just do.

And that kind of shift creates distance—but not from other people. It creates distance from yourself. The version of you that used to operate without hesitation doesn't feel accessible anymore. It's still there somewhere, but you can't reach it the same way. It's like knowing who you are supposed to be but not being able to fully step into it, not being able to trust that it's still there when you need it.

And that uncertainty changes how you move. You start adjusting, not because anyone told you to, but because you don't trust where you stand anymore. I started speaking less and observing more, holding back instead of stepping forward. It wasn't hesitation—it was calculation. Every word, every decision, every interaction felt like something that needed to be measured before I acted on it. I wasn't reacting the way I used to. I was filtering everything first, trying to get it right and trying not to get it wrong. Because I didn't know anymore if the way I used to lead still applied. I didn't know if the instincts I had relied on were still something I could trust. And that doubt didn't stay contained. It spread into everything.

The more I adjusted, the more disconnected I felt, because I wasn't operating the way I knew how. I was trying to operate in a way that felt safer, less noticeable, less exposed. That's a hard place to exist in. On one side, you're still expected to show up, still expected to lead, still expected to perform. The expectations don't change just because something internal has shifted. The role is still there, the responsibilities are still there, and from the outside there's no reason for anyone to think you're not still capable of meeting them.

But on the other side, you're questioning everything. Whether you can. Whether you should. Whether you've already proven that you can't. And the hardest part is that no one else sees that conflict. They still see you the same way they always have—capable, reliable, steady. They respond to you the same way, trust you the same way, and expect the same things from you. Nothing in their behavior reflects what you're experiencing internally, and that creates a gap. A disconnect between how you're seen and how you see yourself. Over time, that gap starts to widen because internally, that's not what it feels like anymore.

It feels like you're holding something together that's already starting to come apart, like you're maintaining an image that no longer matches what's actually happening underneath. The effort it takes to keep that image intact slowly starts to wear on you. Not all at once, just enough day by day until eventually you're not just tired. You're disconnected. Disconnected from the role. Disconnected from the expectations. Disconnected from the version of yourself you used to be.

And that's where the shift really happens. Not in one defining moment. Not in something obvious that everyone can point to. It happens in the space between those moments, where everything still looks the same, but nothing feels like it used to.

The Realization

No one stood in front of me and said it was over. There wasn't a moment when everything stopped, no final call, no ceremony that marked an ending. It wasn't clear, and it wasn't direct. There was no single point I could look back on and say, that's when it happened. It didn't work like that. It was a series of small shifts—subtle changes that, on their own, didn't seem like much, but together added up to something I couldn't ignore anymore. A change in how I felt in situations that used to feel normal. A hesitation where there had never been hesitation before. A quiet awareness that something wasn't lining up the way it used to.

Something had changed, and it wasn't just my situation. It was me.

I could feel it, even if I didn't fully understand it and even if I wasn't ready to accept it. It wasn't something I could explain to anyone else, and it wasn't something I could clearly define. It just existed—constant, present, sitting underneath everything I was doing. The truth was, I hadn't been told I was done. Not yet. As far as anything official went, there was still a chance. There was still a path back, still a version of this where I got it together, pushed through it, and returned to who I had been before. There was still a version of the story where this was just a setback, something temporary, something I could fix if I just worked hard enough.

And I held onto that harder than I probably should have. Because letting go of that hope meant admitting something I wasn't ready to admit. It meant accepting that this wasn't just a phase, that it wasn't something I could simply push through or outwork. It meant acknowledging that the version of myself I was trying to get back to might not be accessible in the way I thought it was. And I wasn't ready for that.

So I stayed in it. I kept showing up. Kept doing what I could. Kept carrying myself the way I thought I was supposed to. I stayed inside the structure because it was familiar, because it gave me something to hold onto while everything else felt uncertain. From the outside, nothing looked different. Everything still fit the role I had always been in. But underneath all of that, something didn't feel the same, and no matter how much I tried to ignore it, it didn't go away.

The harder I tried to hold onto who I had been, the more I felt it slipping away from me. It wasn't something I could point to directly, and it wasn't something I could explain to anyone else. There was no clear evidence I could lay out, no moment I could use to justify it. It was just there, sitting in the background of everything I did. A quiet realization that never really left. Not loud. Not dramatic. Just constant. It didn't interrupt what I was doing, but it never gave me space from it either. It was there when I was working, when I was talking, and when I was trying to focus on anything else. A truth I didn't have the words for yet, but one I couldn't shake.

I knew something was ending, even if I refused to call it that. Even if I kept telling myself this was temporary, that I just needed to get through it, that once I got back to where I was supposed to be, everything would make sense again. Looking back now, that's the part that stands out the most. Not what happened, but how I responded to it. How I could know and still not accept it. How I could feel it and still fight it. How I could be standing in the middle of it and still convince myself it wasn't real.

Because there was no official moment. No paperwork. No final confirmation. Not officially. Not on paper. But internally, I knew my time—as I understood it—was already over, and I still wasn't ready to let it go.

2

The Long Goodbye

Still There, But Not the Same

I was still in Afghanistan. Same place, same people, same mission—at least on paper. From the outside, nothing had really changed. The environment was familiar, the expectations were the same, and everything around me continued moving the way it always had. The rhythm of the deployment didn't slow down just because something had shifted in me. Missions still went out. People still showed up. The system kept moving forward, just like it always does. But it didn't feel the same. Not for me.

There was a separation between what I was surrounded by and what I was experiencing internally. Everything around me still made sense in the way it always had, but I didn't feel connected to it the same way anymore. It was like I was still inside the environment, still moving through it, but not fully part of it. They started having me talk to someone. I don't even remember how it was framed—probably something simple, something routine. Just a conversation. That's how those things always start. Nothing formal, nothing that makes it feel serious. Just an opportunity to sit down and talk. But even that felt different.

I remember sitting there trying to explain something I didn't fully understand myself, trying to put words to a feeling that didn't have a clear shape. I knew something was off, but I couldn't define it in a way that made sense outside of my own head. Every time I tried to explain it, it felt incomplete, like I was circling around something without ever fully getting to it. How do you explain that something feels off when nothing around you has technically changed? Because on the surface, I was fine. I wasn't bleeding. I wasn't injured in a way anyone could point to. There was no visible damage, nothing that would immediately justify what I was feeling. If someone looked at me, there was no reason for them to think anything was wrong. But something wasn't right, and deep down, I knew it.

I talked to my wife. I talked to my kids—or at least I was on the phone with them. I said the things I was supposed to say. I told them I missed them, told them I'd be home soon, asked how they were doing. I went through the motions the way I always had. The conversations sounded the same. The words were the same. From the outside, nothing would have seemed different. But if I'm being honest, I don't know how much of me was actually there in those moments.

There was a distance I couldn't explain. It wasn't physical—I could hear them, they could hear me. The connection was there in that sense. But internally, it felt like something wasn't fully connecting. Like I was present enough to respond, present enough to carry the conversation, but not fully present in the way I should have been. It felt like I was watching myself have those conversations instead of actually living them, like I knew what I was supposed to feel but couldn't fully access it. That's what made it unsettling. The connection was there in words, but not in the way it should have been, and that scared me more than anything else.

Not the panic attacks. Not being grounded. That.

Because if I couldn't feel that—if I couldn't connect to the people who mattered most—then what else was I starting to lose? That question didn't come all at once. It built slowly, sitting underneath everything else and growing the more I became aware of that distance. It wasn't something I could ignore because it showed up in moments that should have felt normal, moments that should have felt grounding. Instead, they felt distant.

And the strange part was, I still had hope. As far as I knew, there was still a chance. Maybe this was temporary. Maybe I'd get cleared. Maybe I'd get back in the seat. Maybe this would all settle down, and I'd return to the version of myself that had always been there before. That belief didn't feel unreasonable. It felt necessary. So I held onto it harder than I probably should have, because letting it go meant facing something I wasn't ready to face yet. It meant acknowledging that this might not be temporary, that this might not resolve in the way I expected it to, and I wasn't ready to step into that reality.

But underneath that hope, there was something else. Something quieter. Something more honest. I knew. Not officially. Not on paper. Not from a commander or a doctor. There was no formal confirmation, no moment when someone told me that this was it. But internally, I knew. And that knowing didn't replace the hope. It existed alongside it, and somehow I carried both of those things at the same time—hope and knowing.

The Flight Home

The flight home was supposed to feel different. That's what everyone tells you. You're going home. You made it. You get to see your family again. It's supposed to be the moment—the release, the relief, the point where everything finally settles and you can breathe again. It's supposed to feel like something. But sitting there, it didn't feel like that.

There was no overwhelming sense of joy, no feeling of completion, no moment where it all hit me the way I thought it would. There wasn't a surge of emotion or a sense of everything finally falling into place. If anything, it felt like the opposite of that. It was just quiet. Not peaceful—just empty in a way I couldn't really explain. It wasn't the kind of quiet that gives you space to relax. It was the kind that leaves you sitting with something you can't quite identify, like there should have been something there—something strong, something meaningful—and instead there was just nothing.

Around me, people were excited. Talking. Laughing. Counting down the hours until we landed. You could feel it in the way they carried themselves, in the way they talked about home, about what they were going to do first, who they were going to see, and what it was going to feel like to finally be back. I remember watching all of it without really feeling part of it. I wasn't disconnected from them physically—I was sitting right there with everyone else—but internally it felt like there was a layer between me and the moment. Like I was observing something I should have been emotionally inside of but couldn't fully reach.

I kept telling myself it would come later. Maybe I just needed time. Maybe it would hit when we landed. Maybe it would hit when I saw my family. Maybe it would hit when I stepped off the plane and everything became real again. I kept waiting for that moment, for that shift, for that feeling everyone talks about, because it had to be there somewhere. It didn't make sense that it wouldn't be. So I convinced myself I just hadn't reached it yet, that whatever was missing would catch up once I was finally home.

But even then, something still felt off. Not in a way I could explain or clearly point to—just enough to know that what I expected to feel wasn't there. And the more I waited for it, the more I started to realize it wasn't simply delayed. It was missing. I had made it back. That part was real. But the feeling that was supposed to come with it never did. I made it back, but I wasn't really there.

The Moment I Thought It Would All Make Sense

We landed, and everything started moving the way it was supposed to. Gear shifted, people stood up, and the energy in the aircraft changed almost immediately. You could feel it—everyone getting ready, everyone anticipating what was waiting on the other side of those doors. There was a weight to it, not heavy in a bad way, just significant. Like everything we had just come out of was about to meet everything we had been away from. This was the moment, the one we had all been moving toward.

We stepped off and formed up, falling into the same structure we had lived in for months. Even that felt familiar—automatic. Line up. Stay in formation. Wait for the next command. It didn't matter where we were. The routine didn't change. My body moved without needing direction, like it didn't know how to do anything else yet. For a second, that felt right, like I still belonged in it. But as we started moving toward the hangar, something inside me shifted. Not fully, just enough to notice. It wasn't strong enough to stop me or pull my attention away from what was happening, but it was there, sitting underneath everything else. A small disconnect I couldn't explain in the moment.

There was excitement. That part was real. I was about to see my wife again. My family. Everything I had been away from for months. This was what it was all for, or at least that's what I told myself. The hangar doors started to open, and everything slowed down. Not literally, but in the way moments stretch when you've built them up in your head for so long that your mind can't quite keep up with reality. The light pushed through first, cutting into the darker space behind us, and then the inside of the hangar came into view—people, movement, families standing there waiting.

My eyes went straight to the crowd. Scanning. Searching. Looking for her. It wasn't controlled or patient. My eyes moved quickly, almost urgently, trying to pick her out of everyone else. Every face I passed over felt like it could be her, and every second that it wasn't felt longer than it should have. There was a brief moment, just a flicker, where a thought crept in: What if she's not here? It didn't make sense, and I pushed it away just as fast as it showed up. I knew she was there. She had to be. I just needed to find her. That was all that mattered in that moment.

But we were still in formation. Still moving. Still waiting. That made it feel like it was taking forever. Every step felt slower than it should have, like something was holding it back. I could feel the pull to break, to move ahead, to just go find her, but that part of me that had been trained to stay in line kept me where I was. Wait. Stay. Follow the process. Even now.

Then the command came. "Fall out." And everything that had been held in place released at once. I didn't think—I moved. Straight to her. I remember closing the distance fast, not caring about anything else around me. Not the people, not the noise, not the movement. Just her. Everything else faded the second I locked onto her, like the rest of the room didn't exist anymore.

When I reached her, I didn't hesitate. I wrapped my arms around her and pulled her in tight, like I needed to make up for all the time in a single moment. I squeezed her harder than I probably realized, like if I let go too soon, something about it wouldn't be real. I kissed her like it was the first time. There was relief in that moment. Real relief. The kind you expect. The kind you're told is coming. For a second, everything lined up the way it was supposed to. Everything felt right. Complete. Like all the distance, all the time, all the separation closed in that one moment. I remember thinking, this is it. This is what it was supposed to feel like.

But underneath that, there was something else. It wasn't loud. It didn't interrupt the moment or take anything away from it. It just sat there, quiet enough to ignore but present enough that it didn't fully go away. A small disconnect, like something didn't land the way I expected it to. Like I was in the moment, but not all the way in it. I didn't understand that at the time. I didn't question it. I didn't stop long enough to figure out what it meant. Everything around me said this was the moment I had been waiting for, so I let it be that. I held onto what made sense—the relief, the excitement, the fact that I was finally home—and ignored everything else.

Looking back on it now, that moment feels different. Not because it wasn't real—it was—but because it wasn't complete. It was the tip of something much bigger, something I couldn't see yet and wasn't ready to understand. It was the beginning of something I was about to run straight into.

What Came After the Hug

For a moment, everything felt the way it was supposed to. We were happy. We rode home together, and that first night—just being in the same place again—felt right. There was a sense of familiarity, of being back where I belonged, of stepping back into something that hadn't changed while I was gone. The conversations were easy. The space felt familiar. Even the quiet felt different than it had overseas. For a moment, it felt like things were finally settling, like maybe that was it. Maybe everything I had been carrying had somewhere to go now that I was home. Maybe the weight I had felt overseas, the things I couldn't explain, the distance I had noticed in myself—maybe all of that was tied to where I had been. And now that I was back, maybe it would stay there.

But it didn't.

It didn't fall apart all at once. There wasn't a single moment where everything shifted or became obvious. If anything, it started in ways that were easy to ignore, small enough that I could brush them off, explain them away, or just avoid thinking about too much. At first, I would lose my train of thought in the middle of a sentence. Not occasionally—enough that I started to notice it. I'd be talking in the middle of a conversation and suddenly it would just be gone. The thought. The point. Everything I was trying to say. I'd sit there for a second trying to find it again, trying to recover something that should have been right there.

There were also moments when I would stop and realize I wasn't fully there. Not in a dramatic way—nothing that would stand out to anyone else—but enough that I could feel it. Like I was present physically, going through the motions, responding when I needed to, but not completely connected to what was happening around me. Like I was still catching up, or maybe never fully arriving. It wasn't constant, but it was consistent, and that made it harder to ignore.

Then there was the drinking. More than usual. More than I needed. At the time, I didn't see it as a problem. I didn't look at it as something that needed to be addressed or controlled. If anything, it felt like a solution. Something that took the edge off just enough to make things feel manageable. It slowed everything down, quieted the background noise, and made it easier to sit still and move through the day without overthinking everything. It gave me just enough space to feel like I was still in control, or at least close to it.

Because technically, I was still in. I was still wearing the uniform. Still showing up. Still doing what I was supposed to do. From the outside, nothing had really changed. I was present. I was functioning. I was meeting expectations in the ways that mattered. It looked like I was holding it together, like I was still fighting and still pushing forward the way I always had.

But underneath that, things were starting to come apart. Not in a way anyone else could see and not in a way I fully understood yet, but enough that I could feel it. And once you feel it, you can't unfeel it.

The High Before the Drop

At work, there were still things I could hold onto. I stepped into a platoon position and had some phenomenal people under me—people who showed up, did their jobs, and made it easier to keep moving forward. They didn't need to be carried the way things had felt overseas. They were solid, dependable, and that mattered more than I realized at the time because it gave me something stable. Something I could still do well.

In that role, things made sense again. There were expectations, responsibilities, and a structure I understood. I knew how to lead. I knew how to show up for them. I knew how to operate in that space, even if everything else felt uncertain. So I leaned into it. Not just because I wanted to, but because I needed to. I went to therapy. I did what they asked. I showed up and tried to work through what was going on, not just for myself, but because I wanted them to see it. I wanted them to see that I was improving, that I was getting stronger, that I was getting back to where I was supposed to be.

Because in my mind, there was still a destination. Back in the air. That was the goal. Not just because I missed flying, but because of what it represented. If I could get back there, then everything else would make sense again. It would mean I was still capable. Still trusted. Still the person I believed myself to be. It would mean none of this had actually taken anything from me.

For a while, I believed it was going to happen. I felt good—focused and motivated in a way I hadn't felt in a long time. There was a sense of direction again, like I wasn't just reacting to what was happening around me but actually moving toward something. Each day felt like progress. Each step forward felt like proof that I was getting back to where I was supposed to be. It felt like control. It felt like I was finding my way back. There was hope, real hope, and that hope carried into everything else.

At home, I was still showing up the way I thought I needed to. I was present, engaged, being the husband and the dad they deserved—or at least that's what it looked like. I was there for the conversations, there for the routines, there for the moments that mattered. From the outside, things held together. The structure was there. The roles were filled. Nothing stood out as being obviously wrong, and I held onto that because as long as it looked right, it felt like maybe it was.

The drinking was still there, but it hadn't taken over. Not yet. It was something I kept in the background, something I could still justify, still manage, still tell myself wasn't a problem. It didn't feel out of control. It felt like something I had control over, something I could use when I needed to and set aside when I didn't. At least, that's what I told myself.

I was still functioning. Still holding it together. Still moving forward. And for a while, it worked. Until it didn't.

Then the first seizure hit.

The First Sting of Betrayal

When I was finally released from the hospital, I thought I was heading home. That's how it was explained to me at first—that I was being transferred to the military hospital on post for continued care. It sounded routine. Controlled. Like a step in the process of getting back to normal. In my head, it meant I was moving forward, that whatever had just happened was behind me and now it was about recovery. And recovery meant getting back. Back to my family. Back to my kids. It had been what felt like a month since I had any real time with them—any moment where I was actually present, actually there. That was the only thing that made sense to me at that point. That was what I held onto. I thought I was going home.

But that's not what happened.

When I got there, things felt different almost immediately. Not in an obvious way—no one sat me down and explained it outright—but there was a shift. A lack of control I hadn't expected. A feeling that something was happening around me that I wasn't fully part of. Then I found out. I wasn't there for routine care. I was being held involuntarily.

That was the first time it felt like something had been taken from me without my understanding or my say in it. It felt like betrayal.

Not because anyone was trying to hurt me, but because I didn't understand it. The decision had been made based on things I didn't remember doing, things I couldn't explain, things that didn't feel like they belonged to me. Things I was told I had said: "I don't want to be here anymore." "Just let it end." "I just want it to stop."

Hearing those words didn't trigger anything in me. No memory. No recognition. There was nothing inside me that connected to them. They felt like they came from someone else entirely. But they came from me, or at least that's what I was told. That disconnect made it worse because it wasn't just about what had happened—it was about not being able to trust my own memory of it. Not being able to stand on anything solid and say, this is what I did, or this is what I felt. I had to rely on what other people told me, and that's a hard place to be.

I was also told that I had tried to fight someone—an assistant who, from what I was told, looked Afghan. That part hit me harder than anything else. Not because of what it meant medically, but because of what it implied about me. I had no memory of it. None. That made it feel even worse because now it wasn't just that I had lost control—it was that I had done things completely outside of who I believed myself to be without any awareness of it. There was no way to reconcile that in the moment. No way to process it other than to feel it.

What I felt first was confusion. Then anxiety. Then something heavier. Because if I was capable of saying those things or doing those things without even knowing it, then what else was I capable of? That question didn't leave. It sat in the background of everything, making it harder to settle, harder to trust myself, harder to feel like I understood what was happening to me.

Instead of feeling like I was moving forward, it felt like I was losing control in a completely different way.

Then, seventy-two hours later, I was released. But by that point there was already a new challenge in front of me, a new reason to fight. I wanted to prove I could still be who they needed me to be, who I believed I was supposed to be. I still had hope for that.

Trying to Prove It Was Still Me

I kept trying to prove it was still me. Not just to other people, but to myself. Because if I could prove it—if I could show that I was still capable, still functioning, still moving in the right direction—then maybe none of this meant what it felt like it meant. Maybe it was temporary. Maybe it was something I could outwork, outlast, or out-discipline the same way I had approached everything else.

So I pushed harder. I leaned into anything that looked like progress. I went to different treatment options, showed up to appointments, and did what I could to make it look like I was moving in the right direction. I said the right things. I followed through on what was asked of me. I did everything I could to demonstrate that I was still engaged in the process and still committed to getting better. I wanted my command to see it—that I was working, that I was improving, that I was getting back to where I needed to be.

Because in my mind, there was still a version of this where I could turn it around. A version where I could get back to who I was before everything started to shift. Not a new version. Not an adjusted one. The same one. The one I trusted. The one I knew. And the closer I thought I was getting to that version, the harder I pushed.

At the same time, though, something else was happening. Something quieter. Something I didn't pay attention to until it was already there. I was drinking more. Staying up later. Pulling away from the things that actually mattered. Not toward my family. Not toward my wife. Toward something smaller. Something contained. Something I could control.

It didn't feel like a conscious decision. There wasn't a moment where I told myself this is what I'm going to do. It just started happening in the background, slowly becoming part of how I got through the day. A way to calm things down. A way to create space when everything felt too loud or too uncertain. Because it wasn't obvious at first, I didn't question it. The more I focused on trying to prove that I was still capable, the more everything else started to slip. Not all at once—just enough. Enough to ignore. Enough to justify. Enough to keep telling myself I still had it under control.

The seizures didn't stop. They kept coming, and I didn't take them as seriously as I should have. I minimized them. I told myself I could manage it, that I had it under control, that it wasn't as bad as it looked from the outside. I convinced myself people were overreacting, that I just needed time, that I just needed to push through.

But I didn't have it under control.

There was one night where it became impossible to ignore. I had a seizure and ended up in the hospital. When they released me, I walked out of the building and had another seizure right there. They still released me. I got in my car, drove home, and ended up wrecking it into a light pole. Somehow, even that still wasn't enough to stop me.

Looking back, that's the part that's hardest to understand. Not what happened, but how far things had to go before I was willing to see it for what it was. How many signs had to show up before I could no longer explain them away. Because my life was starting to fall apart, and I was helping it happen, all while telling myself I was doing everything I could to fix it.

In my head, I wasn't giving up. I wasn't quitting. I was fighting. But what I didn't realize at the time was that I wasn't actually fighting for myself. I was fighting to hold onto something that was already gone.

The Cost At Home

I didn't see what was happening at home. My wife did. She was the one holding everything together, fighting in ways I didn't fully understand at the time. Fighting for me, fighting for our family, making sure things didn't completely fall apart while I was stuck inside something I couldn't see clearly. She was carrying more than I realized—for me, for the kids, for all of us—and she didn't have the option to step away from it.

There was no pause for her. No break. No moment where she could disconnect from what was happening and come back to it later. She was in it every day, every night, dealing with the reality of something I was only partially aware of. And I wasn't meeting her there. I was still focused on myself, on what I was trying to fix, on what I thought I was managing. I was seizing at home. Drinking at home. Living inside a cycle I didn't know how to break while convincing myself I was handling it, convincing myself it wasn't as bad as it looked. It didn't feel like I was dragging anyone else into it. It felt contained, like it was something I was dealing with and would eventually get under control.

But that wasn't the reality.

I wasn't the only one living in it. Every episode. Every night. Every decision I told myself I had under control. They were there for all of it, watching it happen and living inside it alongside me whether I acknowledged it or not. That's the part I didn't understand then—that it didn't stay with me. It didn't stop where I did. It didn't end with my experience of it. It spread quietly at first, in ways that weren't obvious and didn't immediately demand attention, but it spread.

It spread into the house. Into the routines. Into the moments that were supposed to feel normal. Until eventually it became something they had to carry too, and they did it without a choice.

Looking back now, it feels obvious. Clear in a way it never was then. I can see the strain now. I can see what she was holding together. I can see what they were living in. But at the time, I couldn't. I was so focused on who I thought I was supposed to be—so locked into trying to hold onto that version of myself—that I didn't have the awareness to see anything outside of it. Everything was filtered through that lens. Everything came back to whether or not I was getting back to who I thought I needed to be.

Because of that, I missed what was right in front of me. Not just what it was doing to me, but what it was doing to them. My focus narrowed until everything became smaller and smaller, until eventually it came down to the next drink and the bottom of a bottle.

The Moment It Was Taken Out of My Hands

"Your options are either a med board or a medical chapter. I wish I had more options, but that's where we are at."

Those words have stayed with me. Not just because of what they meant, but because of how final they felt. There wasn't space in them. No room to negotiate, no room to push back, no room to prove anything different. It wasn't framed as a possibility or a discussion. It was an outcome. In that moment, it stopped being something I could fight through. It wasn't something I could outwork or push past anymore. It wasn't a matter of effort or discipline. It wasn't something I could fix by showing up earlier, trying harder, or proving that I still had it. It was already decided, and there was nothing I could do to change it.

That was the part that hit the hardest. Not the words themselves, but the lack of control behind them. What I felt in that moment wasn't anger, at least not in the way I expected. It wasn't loud or reactive. It was something quieter and heavier, something closer to betrayal. Not because they were wrong, and not because the decision didn't make sense, but because the system I had put so much faith in wasn't what I thought it was. Or maybe it was, and I just didn't understand it until I was standing on the other side of it.

I had told people to trust it. To use it. To speak up, to say what was on their mind, and to get help when they needed it. I had told them the system would take care of them, that they didn't have to carry everything on their own. That's what I believed. That's what I told others. Now I was sitting there hearing those words and realizing I had to face all of that from the other side—not as the one giving the guidance, but as the one being processed through it. And it felt different.

The hope I had been holding onto—getting back in the air, getting back to who I was—didn't matter anymore. That path wasn't just unlikely. It was gone. I didn't know what replaced it. There was no immediate next step that felt real. No clear direction to shift toward. Just the absence of something that had defined me for so long, with nothing solid in its place yet.

What hit me wasn't even pain. It was numbness. A kind of emptiness that didn't come with a clear emotion attached to it, just a sense that something had been taken away and there was nothing left to fill the space it left behind. It didn't feel dramatic. It didn't feel overwhelming. It just felt gone.

The feeling of betrayal didn't fully make sense to me at the time, but I could feel that it had changed something in how I saw things, in how I trusted things, and in how I understood where I fit in all of it. I couldn't look at people the same after that. I couldn't look at the system the same. I couldn't even look at myself the same.

Because in my mind, it didn't just mean I was done. It meant something about me. It meant I had failed. Failed as a pilot. Failed as a leader. Failed as someone who was supposed to be able to handle it. Once that thought settled in, it didn't go anywhere. It stayed. It followed me into everything that came after, shaping how I saw myself, shaping how I responded to things, and shaping what I believed I was worth.

I felt like a failure. Whatever word someone else might use for it, that's what it felt like inside me.

3

Crack In the Armor

Identity Destruction Starts With a Crack

I was still in, at least on paper. I was still wearing the uniform, still drawing a paycheck, still carrying the rank—CPT Padilla. From the outside, nothing had fully separated yet. Everything that had defined me for years was still technically there, still attached to my name, still something people could see and recognize. But that was all it was at that point: a name, a title, something I could put on, but not something I felt connected to anymore.

Behind it, there was nothing. No role. No responsibility. No place I actually fit into. I was at WTB, and for the first time in my career, I wasn't leading, wasn't flying, and wasn't responsible for anything beyond just existing. There were no decisions that depended on me, no people looking to me for direction, and no structure that required me to show up in the way I always had before. That was something I didn't know how to do.

Everything I had built myself around had been tied to purpose, responsibility, and being part of something that required something from me. Without that, there was no reference point. Most of my time was spent at home trying to figure out what that even looked like, trying to understand how to exist without the structure I had always relied on. What was left didn't feel like enough. It felt empty.

It also felt like I was a fraud, like I was still wearing something I hadn't earned anymore. Like at any moment someone was going to look at me and realize I didn't belong there, that the uniform didn't match who I was anymore. The more I sat in that feeling, the worse it got because there was nothing to counter it. Nothing to prove it wrong. Just time and space to sit with it.

The days started blending together. There was no real schedule, no real direction, just waking up, existing, and waiting for the day to end. Somewhere along the way, the drinking stopped feeling like a decision and started feeling like part of the routine. Not something I questioned, just something I did.

I remember one night in particular. Nothing big had happened that day. No trigger. No event. No reason I could point to. That was the worst part about it—it didn't take anything anymore. I was just sitting there alone, drink in hand, telling myself it was only to take the edge off. That's what it always was at first. Just enough to quiet things down.

But one turned into another, and then another. Somewhere in the middle of it, I stopped paying attention to how much I was actually drinking. The room didn't spin, at least not at first, but everything felt dulled. Like I wasn't fully in it, but I also wasn't far enough removed from it to escape it either. Just stuck in the middle.

I remember sitting there thinking, this isn't who I am. Right behind that thought came another one: Then who the hell are you?

I didn't have an answer.

That was the part that hit the hardest. Not the drinking. Not the situation. The fact that I couldn't answer something that used to feel so clear.

The drinking didn't stop. If anything, it became easier to justify. I was still getting paid, still showing up just enough to avoid drawing attention, still technically meeting the baseline of what was expected. So I drank more. More often. More consistently. Eventually, it became part of the routine instead of something I questioned.

The seizures followed the same pattern. They got heavier, more frequent, and less predictable. Instead of seeing them for what they were, I ignored them or convinced myself I could manage them. I told myself I just needed time, that I would figure it out, that this was something I could still get control of if I just kept pushing. Because that's what I had always done.

Underneath all of that, though, something else was building. I was angry. At the situation. At the system. At myself. It wasn't loud or obvious, and it didn't come out in any clear or controlled way. It stayed internal, sitting there and building over time, turning in on itself until it started shaping how I saw everything, including who I was becoming.

The longer I stayed in that space, the less I recognized myself. Not just in what I was doing, but in how I was thinking, how I was reacting, and how I was existing. I wasn't becoming a version of who I used to be. I was becoming someone I had never wanted to be, and I didn't know how to stop it.

Falling With Nothing to Catch Me

There was no structure left. No schedule telling me where to be, no expectations beyond the bare minimum, no mission pulling me forward or responsibility demanding my attention. Everything that used to give my day shape was gone, and what replaced it wasn't freedom or rest. It was just time, and I didn't know what to do with it.

For so long, every part of my day had been accounted for. There was always something to prepare for, something to execute, something that required my focus. Even when things were hard, there was direction. There was movement. There was a reason to get up and engage with what was in front of me, even on the days when I didn't want to. That structure didn't just organize my time. It gave me a place to exist, a way to measure myself, and a way to know I was still doing something that mattered.

Now there wasn't.

I would wake up without a clear reason to get moving. No urgency. No immediate purpose. Just the weight of another day that I had to figure out on my own. On the surface, that sounds simple, maybe even appealing. Time off. Space to recover. A chance to slow down after everything that had come before.

But it didn't feel like that.

When you're used to operating at a certain level—when your identity is built around being needed—having nothing in front of you doesn't feel like rest. It doesn't feel like relief. It feels like you've been removed from something you were supposed to be part of. Like you've been set aside. Like everything that gave you value has been stripped down to the point where you don't know what's left.

That's where things started to shift.

There were days where I would just sit there longer than I should have. Not doing anything. Not because there wasn't anything I could do, but because nothing felt important enough to start. I would look around knowing I should get up, knowing I should move, knowing I should do something with the time in front of me, and I just wouldn't.

It wasn't laziness. It wasn't even a conscious decision. It felt more like there was no internal push anymore, no reason strong enough to override the stillness. The longer I sat there, the heavier it became—not physically, but mentally. Like the effort it would take to break that stillness kept increasing the longer I stayed in it. Once you don't start, it becomes easier not to start again.

Without something external demanding my attention, everything internal started getting louder. What used to be background noise—doubt, questions, things I didn't want to think about—now had space to show up. Not just show up, but stay. There was nothing redirecting my focus anymore. Nothing interrupting it. It just sat there, and the more time I had, the more it filled it.

What used to feel like structure had been replaced with empty space, and that space didn't give me room to recover. It gave everything I had been avoiding somewhere to live. The thoughts, the uncertainty, the realization that I didn't know who I was supposed to be without everything I had built myself around—it all started settling in.

I didn't have an answer for any of it.

The longer I stayed in that space, the harder it became to separate myself from it. Not in some dramatic or obvious way, but in something quieter. Something that built slowly over time. A gradual shift from dealing with it to living inside it.

Once that line started to blur, it became harder to find my way back out. Because without structure, without direction, and without something pulling me forward, there was nothing there to catch me.

No Safe Space

There was no structure left. No schedule telling me where to be, no expectations beyond the bare minimum, no mission pulling me forward or responsibility demanding my attention. Everything that used to give my day shape was gone, and what replaced it wasn't relief. It was just time, and I didn't know what to do with it.

For so long, every part of my day had been accounted for. There was always something to prepare for, something to execute, something that needed my focus. Even when things were difficult, there was direction. There was movement. There was a place to put my energy, a way to move forward even when I didn't feel like I had it in me. That structure didn't just organize my time. It gave me a place to exist inside of it. It gave me something to step into, something that made sense whether I felt ready for it or not.

Now there wasn't.

I would wake up without a reason to get moving. No urgency. No direction. Just the weight of another day that I had to figure out on my own. On the surface, that sounds simple. It sounds like something people would want, something that should feel like a break or a chance to recover. But it wasn't.

When your identity is built around being needed, having nothing in front of you doesn't feel like rest. It doesn't feel like relief. It feels like you've been removed. Like you've been set aside and disconnected from the thing that used to give you purpose. When that purpose disappears, it doesn't leave space behind. It leaves a gap you don't know how to fill.

I could feel that gap every day.

There were moments where I would sit there longer than I should have, knowing I needed to get up, knowing I needed to do something—anything—and I just wouldn't. Not because I didn't care and not because I didn't know better, but because nothing in front of me felt important enough to move toward. There was no pull. No urgency. No reason strong enough to break the stillness.

The longer I stayed in that stillness, the heavier it became. Not physically, but mentally. Like the effort it would take to get up kept increasing the longer I stayed where I was. Once you don't start, it becomes easier not to start again.

Without that structure, there was nowhere to put what was building inside me. Work used to be the place where I could focus. The mission used to be the place where I could channel everything I didn't want to deal with. Even the chaos had structure to it. It gave me something to move toward, something to react to, something that kept everything else at a distance. It didn't solve anything, but it kept it contained.

Now there was no distance.

There was no place to go where things felt clear. No role to step into that made everything else quiet down. No space that felt controlled. What used to be separated—what I could once compartmentalize—was now all in the same place, all at once.

Everywhere felt the same.

The more time I had to sit in that, the harder it became to ignore what was already there. The thoughts didn't have anything to compete with anymore. The doubt didn't have anything to push against. It didn't come and go. It stayed. Constant. Present. Filling the space that used to be occupied by something else.

There was nowhere to redirect it. Nowhere to outrun it. There was no safe space. The longer I sat in that, the more it started to get to me.

Coping In The Worst Ways

Home didn't feel the way I thought it would. I was there physically—sitting in the same rooms, having the same conversations, going through the motions I knew I was supposed to. From the outside, everything looked familiar. The environment hadn't changed. My wife was still there. My kids were still there. The life I had worked so hard to build was still right in front of me, unchanged in all the ways that should have made it feel stable. But it didn't feel the same, and I didn't feel like I belonged in it the way I used to.

I wasn't showing up the same way. Not fully, and not consistently. There were moments where I could feel it, where I could see them clearly, hear them, and be present in the way I knew I was supposed to be. Moments where things felt real again, where I felt like myself, even if only for a short time. In those moments, it felt like maybe I hadn't lost it completely, like maybe I was still there underneath everything else. But those moments didn't last. Just as quickly as they showed up, they would fade, and I'd find myself sitting there again—physically present but mentally somewhere else.

There was a distance I couldn't explain, like I was watching everything happen instead of actually living it. I knew what I should be feeling. I knew what those moments were supposed to mean. I just couldn't stay connected to them long enough for it to feel real. That's what made it worse. It wasn't ignorance. It was awareness. I could see it happening in real time—the disconnect, the inconsistency, the way I would drift in and out of moments that mattered. I could feel the gap between who I was supposed to be and how I was actually showing up. The more I noticed it, the harder it became to ignore.

I knew they could feel it too, even if they didn't say it. Even if they tried to adjust around it and meet me where I was without forcing anything, that kind of distance doesn't stay hidden. It shows up in the small things—the conversations that don't go anywhere, the reactions that don't match the moment, the way you start pulling back without even realizing you're doing it. It shows up in what's missing.

The more aware I became of that, the harder it was to face. I knew what it was supposed to feel like. I knew what they deserved. I knew what I used to be able to give without even thinking about it. And I knew I wasn't giving them that.

That awareness didn't pull me closer. It pushed me further away. Because it's one thing to struggle. It's another thing to see it clearly and still not know how to fix it. Instead of leaning into it, I started finding ways to avoid it.

Fighting a Losing Battle

There was no structure left. No schedule telling me where to be, no expectations beyond the bare minimum, no mission pulling me forward or responsibility demanding my attention. Everything that used to give my day shape was gone, and what replaced it wasn't rest—it was just time. And I didn't know what to do with it.

For so long, every part of my day had been accounted for. There was always something to prepare for, something to execute, something that required my attention. Even when things were difficult, there was direction. There was a reason to engage, a reason to move, a reason to keep pushing forward. That structure didn't just organize my time—it gave me a way to measure myself, a way to know I was still doing something that mattered.

Now there wasn't.

I would wake up without a clear reason to get moving. No urgency, no direction—just the weight of another day I had to figure out on my own. And on the surface, that sounds simple, like something that should feel like a break, like time to recover after everything that had happened.

But it didn't.

Because when you're used to operating at a certain level—when your entire identity is built around being needed—having nothing in front of you doesn't feel like relief. It feels like you've been removed from something you were supposed to be part of. Like you've been set aside, disconnected from the system that once gave you purpose. And when that connection is gone, it doesn't leave you with clarity—it leaves you with questions you don't have answers to.

And even though I tried to adjust to that, it never really settled. I would tell myself I just needed time, that I would figure it out, that I would find some kind of rhythm again. I tried to approach it the same way I had approached everything else—by pushing through, by staying disciplined, by convincing myself that effort alone would be enough to get me back to where I was.

But this wasn't something I could push through.

The more I tried to force structure where there wasn't any, the more obvious it became that I didn't have anything solid to anchor myself to. There was nothing to stabilize against, nothing to measure progress against, nothing that told me I was moving in the right direction. Without that feedback, without that sense of forward movement, it became harder to trust anything I was doing.

And slowly, that started to wear on me.

Because it didn't feel like I was taking a step back to recover.

It felt like I was losing ground.

And the harder I tried to fight that feeling, the more it stayed. Not because I wasn't trying hard enough, but because I was trying to solve it the only way I knew how—with effort, with discipline, with control—without realizing that none of those things applied the same way anymore.

And no matter how much I told myself I was still fighting...

it started to feel like I was fighting something against which I couldn't win.

The Quiet Ending

I tried to escape it. Not in any clear or intentional way—nothing that felt like a decision I could point to later. It wasn't something I planned or justified in the moment. It was just whatever worked, whatever made things feel a little quieter and a little more manageable. I wasn't thinking about where it was leading or what it was becoming. I was just trying to get through the day without having to sit with everything that was building underneath it.

The drinking never really left. If anything, it became easier. There was no structure stopping it, no immediate consequence I was willing to acknowledge, and no reason strong enough in the moment to hold me back. So I leaned into it. One drink turned into more, more turned into routine, and before long it became something I didn't question anymore. It didn't feel like a choice. It felt like part of the day, part of how I moved through it, or at least that's what I told myself.

As long as I stayed occupied—whether it was drinking, staying up late, or keeping my mind somewhere else—I didn't have to sit with what was actually going on. I didn't have to think about what I had lost or what I was becoming. I didn't have to deal with the gap between who I thought I was supposed to be and who I was starting to feel like. I could keep everything at a distance just long enough to avoid dealing with it directly.

That distance started to feel normal. Not in a way I was aware of at first, but in the way it slowly became the default. The more I avoided it, the easier it became to keep avoiding it. The more space I created, the less I had to confront anything that didn't make sense. It wasn't fixing anything. It was just delaying it, pushing it further out of reach while it continued building underneath everything else.

For a while, that felt easier. Not better. Just easier. But it didn't fix anything. It didn't change what was happening underneath the surface. It just created more space—space between me and reality, between me and the people around me, and eventually between me and myself. The things that used to feel closest started to feel distant. The things that used to ground me didn't carry the same weight anymore.

The longer I stayed in that space, the harder it became to come back out of it. Not because I didn't want to, but because I didn't know where to start. There wasn't a clear way back. Just the awareness that I had drifted further than I meant to, and no real sense of how to reverse it. By that point, I wasn't really trying to escape it anymore. I was already in it.

4

Becoming Someone I Didn't Recognize

A Glimpse of Something Like Hope

I didn't find out I was out of the Army the way I thought I would. There wasn't a conversation. No sit-down, no explanation, no moment where someone walked me through what was happening or what it meant. There was no transition point I could look back on and say, that's when it ended. No finality I could attach meaning to. Instead, I found out in a way that didn't feel real at first. My paycheck didn't hit.

I remember looking at my account, thinking something was off, assuming it had to be delayed or some kind of mistake. That had to be it. There was no way something that big would just stop without anyone saying anything. So I checked again. Waited. Tried to make sense of it. But it wasn't a mistake.

That was it. That was how I found out.

After everything—after the deployments, the responsibility, the years of doing what I was supposed to do—that's how it ended. Not with a conversation. Not with clarity. Not even with acknowledgment. Just nothing. Somehow, that wasn't even the end of it.

I was told I still had to out-process. Even though I was already out, even though on paper it had already been decided, I still had to go through the steps. Turn things in. Sign paperwork. Close it out properly. I remember thinking how disconnected that felt, how I was supposed to bring closure to something I hadn't even been told had ended. How do you close something you didn't know was already over? It didn't feel real. It didn't feel right.

It felt like I had been cut out of my own life without being told.

What made it harder wasn't just how it ended. It was what came after.

My old battalion reached out. They wanted to present me with an award, recognition for what I had done, for my time, for my service. On paper, it was everything I had worked toward, everything that should have meant something.

I couldn't bring myself to accept it.

Not because it didn't matter, but because I couldn't separate the recognition from how everything had ended. All I could see was how it felt. The way I found out. The way it was handled. The way I was left trying to make sense of something that had already been decided without me. It all sat there tied together, and I couldn't pull one piece away from the rest.

Underneath all of that, there was anger. Not loud. Not something I expressed outwardly. Just steady. Sitting there, not moving. It wasn't directed at one person, and it wasn't something I could point at and say, that's the reason. It was broader than that. Something that came from the gap between what I believed things were supposed to be and what they actually were.

So I said no.

I didn't want the award. I didn't want the recognition. I didn't want anything tied to it. At that point, it didn't feel like something to be proud of. It felt like something that had been taken from me, and I didn't know what to do with that.

Trying to Hold it Together

I thought things might finally start to turn. I got offered a job right out of the Army, working in the safety department for my city. For the first time in a while, it felt like I had direction again, like there was something in front of me to step into instead of just something I had lost behind me. It wasn't the same as what I had done before, and it didn't carry the same identity or weight, but it was something. Something steady. Something that gave me a reason to get up and move forward instead of just trying to get through the day.

For a moment, that felt like hope.

It felt like maybe I could rebuild something. Not the same version of what I had lost, but something close enough to stand on. Something that could give shape to the days again, something that could pull me out of the space I had been sitting in. I told myself this was a step forward, that this was what moving on was supposed to look like.

At home, life was moving forward too. My wife was pregnant with our third child, and that should have been something I could fully lean into, something I could be present for in a way that grounded everything else. It should have been something that pulled me back into what mattered most and gave everything else perspective.

But this one was different.

It was harder in ways I wasn't prepared for. There were moments where I thought I might lose her, moments where I thought we might lose the baby. Times where things didn't feel stable, where everything felt uncertain again in a way that I couldn't control. That lack of control brought something back that I had already been struggling with: the feeling that no matter what I did, I couldn't stabilize the things that mattered most.

Thankfully, they were okay.

That didn't mean it didn't affect me.

That kind of fear doesn't just disappear when the moment is over. It stays with you. It lingers in the background, shaping how you think, how you move, and how you respond to everything around you. It doesn't stay contained to those moments. It carries forward, adding weight to things that are already heavy. When you're already operating from a place where everything feels unstable, that extra weight doesn't settle evenly. It compounds.

Instead of grounding me, it pushed me further into everything I was already struggling to manage.

I didn't have a way to process it. I didn't have a way to separate it from everything else that was already building. Instead of dealing with it directly, it just became part of the pressure. Part of the background. Part of the weight I was carrying into everything else.

I didn't handle that well.

The Crash

At work, I tried to show up. Tried to be what I thought I was supposed to be. From the outside, it probably looked like I was doing it. I was there. I was present enough to get through the day, complete what was in front of me, and meet expectations at a basic level. But it wasn't the same. It wasn't consistent. It wasn't grounded in anything that felt stable. It was effort—constant effort to hold something together that didn't feel like it was holding.

Underneath all of that, everything was still there.

The drinking didn't stop. The late nights didn't stop. The thoughts didn't slow down. If anything, they followed me into it. Into the workday. Into conversations. Into moments where I was supposed to be focused on something in front of me, but part of me was somewhere else entirely. The more I tried to function like things were normal, the more everything started to bleed through.

Not in obvious ways at first. Just enough to feel it.

There were moments where I wasn't fully present. Moments where I had to work harder than I should have just to keep up. Moments where I could feel the disconnect between what I was doing and where I actually was mentally. Because I wasn't just dealing with what was happening in front of me. I was still chasing something behind me.

The version of myself I used to be.

The one I thought I should still be.

The more I chased that version, the further away it felt. Every attempt to show up the way I used to only highlighted the difference between who I was then and who I was now. It wasn't closing the gap. It was making it more obvious.

That gap kept getting wider. Wider between what I expected of myself and what I was actually capable of in that moment. Wider between how I was seen and how I felt. Wider between the life I was trying to step into and the one I couldn't let go of.

The harder I tried to bridge it, the more it felt like I was losing ground.

The Cost At Home

Eventually, it caught up to me. Not all at once and not in a way that felt dramatic or sudden, but in small shifts that became harder and harder to ignore. It showed up in the details—missed focus, inconsistency, moments where I wasn't as present or reliable as I needed to be. Things that might have been manageable on their own started to add up, and over time they became something I couldn't cover or push through the way I had before.

At first, it was subtle. Easy to explain away. A bad day. A rough night. Just needing to reset. But those explanations didn't hold for long. The pattern started repeating, and the space between those moments got smaller. What used to feel like isolated slips started feeling consistent, like something I couldn't outrun by simply showing up and trying harder the next day.

I tried to keep it together. I told myself I just needed to lock back in, focus, and get back to the level I knew I was capable of. I leaned on what had always worked—discipline, effort, pushing through—but it wasn't enough. This wasn't something that responded to effort alone. It wasn't something I could muscle my way through or correct by forcing myself back into it.

The gap between where I was and where I needed to be kept growing, and the more aware I became of it, the harder it was to ignore. Because it wasn't just about performance anymore. It was about who I was in that space.

Eventually, it became clear that I couldn't close that gap. Not the way I was trying to. Not by pretending it wasn't there, and not by pushing harder. Once that realization settled in, everything I had been holding together at work started giving way. Not in a dramatic collapse and not in something that forced immediate attention, but in something quieter. Something that simply stopped working the way it used to.

It didn't collapse all at once. It just stopped holding. Once that went, there wasn't much left for me to stand on.

When It Finally Broke

By that point, what I had left was drinking, and my family paid for it.

I left my wife to carry everything during one of the hardest pregnancies we had faced. She was dealing with uncertainty, fear, and the weight of holding the family together, and I wasn't there in the way I needed to be. I wasn't helping. I wasn't steady. I wasn't showing up for our kids the way they needed me to. From the outside, I was still in the house, still part of the routine, but in every way that actually mattered, I wasn't where I needed to be.

That absence wasn't neutral. It had weight. It shifted everything around it, and it didn't stop there.

I was spending money we didn't have, making decisions without thinking about what they would cost us later, and moving through life in a way that felt disconnected from everything I had built before. It didn't feel intentional in the moment. It felt like I was just getting through the day, just trying to manage what was in front of me. Looking back now, though, it was clear how far off I had drifted.

It didn't feel like me. It felt like I was stuck inside something I didn't recognize, like I was watching myself make choices that didn't line up with who I had been and not knowing how to stop it. There was a disconnect between awareness and action. I could see pieces of it, but not enough to interrupt it, and the more it happened, the more normal it started to feel.

People around me saw it. My mother-in-law saw it. Others saw it too. They tried to say something, tried to step in, and tried to get me to see what was happening before it got any worse. They weren't guessing. They weren't overreacting. They were seeing it clearly, even when I couldn't.

But I didn't listen. Not because I didn't care, but because I couldn't separate what they were saying from what I felt like I needed in the moment. In my head, what I was doing gave me some sense of control. It was something I could turn to, something I could rely on, something that gave me relief, even if it was temporary and even if it came at the cost of everything else.

That's the part I didn't understand then. What felt like control was actually the thing taking it away. By the time I could finally see it clearly, the damage was already there.

Becoming Someone I Didn't Recognize

Eventually, it broke again.

"I can't have the kids watch you destroy yourself anymore. I'm taking them to my hometown."

Those words landed in a way I couldn't ignore. There wasn't an argument to make, nothing to push back on, and nothing I could say that would have changed what was already clear. It wasn't said out of anger. It wasn't emotional or reactive. It was steady. Final. The kind of decision that doesn't come from one moment, but from everything that led up to it.

I knew she was right.

I didn't fight it because there was nothing to fight. She was doing what any good mother would do. Protecting what mattered most. Protecting them from something I hadn't been able to control. Protecting them from me. That was something I couldn't argue with, even if hearing it forced me to confront things I had spent a long time avoiding.

So I helped.

I helped find a place for them. Helped pack. Helped move things forward. I did what needed to be done the same way I always had when something needed to get handled. I stayed in motion, stayed focused on the task, and stayed inside that familiar space where there was something to execute.

But this time it was different.

I wasn't fixing anything. I was helping carry out a decision that had been made because of me.

There's a different kind of weight in that. Not the kind you push through and not the kind you absorb for someone else. The kind you have to sit with because you know exactly why it's happening. There was no confusion. No misunderstanding. Just clarity.

The hardest part wasn't even the separation. It was knowing she hadn't given up. She was still holding onto something I couldn't see anymore. Still waiting for me to wake up. Still believing there was a version of me that would come back to who I had been. That belief was still there for her, even when it wasn't there for me.

I could see it.

I just couldn't meet her there.

I didn't turn it around. I didn't step into the version of myself she still believed in. If anything, I got worse.

Running Instead of Fixing It

She was trying to rebuild. Trying to find her identity again, trying to create some kind of stability for our kids, and trying to put something back together after everything we had been through. There was movement in her direction—forward, even if it was slow and difficult.

I was moving the other way.

I wasn't helping. I wasn't leading. I wasn't even really present. I was just there, existing in the same space without actually contributing to it. It didn't feel intentional in the moment. It just felt like I didn't have anything left to give. Looking back now, though, it was clear how far I had drifted from the person I used to be.

I didn't recognize myself anymore.

I was on so many medications that I couldn't tell what was doing what. The VA was giving me everything they thought might help, adjusting things, trying different combinations, and I didn't understand any of it. I didn't question it either. I just took what they gave me and kept moving through the day the only way I knew how.

Numb. Angry. Disconnected.

I stayed there longer than I should have.

As much as I told myself I didn't have control over what was happening, the truth was more complicated than that. I wasn't just stuck. I was avoiding. Avoiding the possibility of trying and failing again. Avoiding the chance that I might make things worse if I actually stepped in and tried to change anything.

So instead, I stayed where I was, even though that was already making things worse.

Alone in Colorado

I moved into a small one-bedroom apartment. There was no family there, no structure beyond work, and no one around to anchor anything outside of what I chose to do with my time. It was just me, alone in a space that felt empty in a way I hadn't experienced before. Not just quiet, but still. There was no background noise, no movement, no interruptions. No one asking anything of me, no one depending on me, and no one there to notice how I was showing up—or not showing up.

It was just me and whatever I brought with me.

What I brought with me ended up being the same things I had been trying to outrun the entire time. The drinking followed me. The need for distraction stayed. The isolation that had been building didn't go away. It just had more room now. There was nothing pushing back against it, nothing forcing me to step outside of it, and nothing interrupting the pattern once it started. There was no reason to stop, no moment that required me to shift, and no external pressure strong enough to break the cycle.

Without that pressure, it settled in.

Not all at once and not in a way that felt dramatic or noticeable, but gradually, day by day, until it became part of the environment. Something I moved through without thinking about it. Something that didn't stand out because there was nothing else there to contrast it against.

After a while, that became normal. Not something I questioned and not something I saw as temporary. Just the way things were.

The days blurred together. The routines—if you could even call them that—started revolving around whatever kept things quiet and whatever kept me from sitting still too long. There wasn't anything pulling me forward, and there wasn't anything behind me that I felt like I could go back to. There was only space, and I filled it the only way I knew how.

The longer I stayed in it, the less it felt like something happening to me and the more it started to feel like who I was.

5

The Way Back

The Turning Point

At some point, being alone stopped feeling like relief and started feeling like something I couldn't ignore.

The apartment didn't change. The routine didn't change. The way I was living didn't suddenly fall apart in some obvious way. If anything, it stayed exactly the same, and that was the problem. There was nothing interrupting it, nothing forcing me to look at it differently, and nothing pushing me to step outside of it. Every day rolled into the next, and after a while it stopped feeling like time was moving forward and started feeling like I was just sitting inside something that wasn't going anywhere.

For a while, I told myself that was fine. That this was what life was supposed to look like now. No chaos. No pressure. No immediate responsibility. Just space. But something started to feel off. It wasn't loud or dramatic, and it wasn't something I could clearly point to and say this is what's wrong. It was quieter than that. Just a feeling that sat in the background, showing up more often than it used to. A moment here, a thought there—small enough to brush off, but consistent enough that it never fully went away.

It showed up in the silence, in the moments where there was nothing to distract me, in the pauses between everything else. Those small gaps where there was no noise, no movement, and nothing pulling my attention in a specific direction—that's where it lived. Every time it showed up, I treated it the same way I had been treating everything else that didn't have an easy answer. I pushed past it. I filled the space with something else. Turned something on, grabbed a drink, and found anything that would keep me from sitting there long enough to let it settle in. I stayed inside the same patterns and told myself there was no reason to change anything, that this was just how things were now and that I had already adjusted to it.

But I hadn't.

That became harder to ignore.

Until one night.

It didn't start any differently than the others. I went to a bar I had started to feel comfortable in. Same place, same kind of night, same reason for being there. It wasn't about anything specific anymore. It was just what I did. A way to pass time, a way to stay occupied, and a way to keep everything from getting too quiet. There was something about being there that made things easier. Not better. Just easier. The noise, the movement, and the presence of other people created just enough distance between me and everything going on inside my head that I didn't have to deal with it directly. I could exist inside it without thinking too much about why I was there or what I was avoiding.

For a while, that worked.

Until it didn't.

That night went further than it should have, but it didn't feel like that in the moment. It built the way it always did—slow and steady, one drink turning into another, each one making it easier not to think about how many there had already been. There wasn't a point where I stopped and said this is too much. There wasn't a moment where I recognized I had crossed a line. There was just a point where I stopped paying attention.

After that, there's nothing. No memory of leaving. No memory of the drive. No sense of transition from one place to the other. Just a gap where something should have been.

Then I woke up face down on my living room floor.

For a moment, nothing made sense. There was that split second where I didn't know where I was, didn't know what position I was in, and didn't even fully recognize what I was looking at. It felt like waking up inside a situation without any context, like I had been dropped into the middle of something without understanding how I got there. Then things slowly started coming back. Not in a way that filled in the gap—just enough to realize there was one.

I pushed myself up, trying to get my bearings and figure out what had happened. My head felt heavy, not just from the drinking, but from the absence of anything to connect to. I looked around the apartment expecting something—anything—that would explain how I got there. But there was nothing. No memory to match it. No clear sign. Just empty space where it should have been.

I started moving around without really thinking about it, checking things and looking for something that made sense. It wasn't even intentional. It was automatic, like my brain was trying to find something solid to grab onto, something that would make the situation feel real again. That's when I found my wallet outside near my truck. That was the only reason I knew I made it home, because there was no other explanation.

Standing there holding it and trying to piece everything together, I kept waiting for something to click. Some version of the night to come back. Some sequence of events that would make it make sense. But nothing came. There was no way to explain it. No way to justify it. No way to tell myself I still had control over it.

That was what finally hit me. Not because something dramatic had happened, and not because there was damage I could point to or consequences I could clearly see, but because I couldn't account for it. I couldn't trust myself to know what I had done or how I had gotten there. Up until that point, no matter how bad things felt, I had still believed I had control, or at least enough of it to pull things back if I needed to. Enough to stay within some kind of boundary, even if I got close to it.

But this wasn't that.

This wasn't pushing limits.

This was losing track of them completely.

Standing there trying to make sense of something I couldn't explain, I realized something I hadn't fully allowed myself to see before. I didn't have control. Not in the way I thought I did, and not in the way I needed to. Once that realization showed up, it didn't leave. It sat underneath everything else, impossible to ignore. The more I thought about it, the heavier it became, because if I couldn't trust myself with something as basic as getting home, what else couldn't I trust?

That question didn't come with an answer. Just a realization.

Something had to change.

The First Real Decision

That was the moment I decided something had to change.

Not perfectly, and not all at once. I wasn't suddenly clear or back in control, and I didn't have some structured plan for how to fix everything. There wasn't a roadmap and no set of steps I could follow to get back to where I thought I needed to be. I didn't wake up the next day with clarity or direction. If anything, I woke up with more questions than answers. But I knew one thing for certain: it couldn't keep going the way it was.

What had been happening wasn't sustainable, and for the first time I couldn't ignore that anymore. It wasn't just a thought I could push aside or something I could bury under routine or distraction. It was there, sitting in front of me in a way that didn't leave room for anything else. Even though I didn't know what the right move was, I knew doing nothing wasn't an option anymore.

So I started with what I thought I could control. At that point, control didn't mean having everything figured out. It didn't mean confidence or clarity. It meant finding one thing—anything—that felt like it belonged to me again.

The medications had become something I didn't understand. I didn't know what I was taking, what was helping, what was hurting, or what wasn't doing anything at all. It had turned into something I followed without thinking, something that felt like it was happening to me instead of something I had any say in. I was taking them because I was told to, because it was part of the process, because it was what I was supposed to do. But I didn't feel connected to it, and I didn't feel like I understood it. That didn't sit right anymore.

Up until that point, everything had felt like it was outside of me—decisions being made, outcomes happening, things moving forward whether I understood them or not. It felt like I was just along for it, reacting to whatever came next instead of having any real say in it. After everything that had already happened, that lack of control wasn't something I could keep accepting the same way. I needed something that felt like mine, even if it wasn't perfect and even if it wasn't the right way to do it.

So I made a decision.

I stopped.

Cold turkey.

There wasn't a long buildup to it. No drawn-out internal debate. No moment where I sat down and mapped it out. It was simpler than that. It was a line I decided to draw, even if I didn't fully understand what was on the other side of it. Looking back, it probably wasn't the smartest way to do it. It wasn't planned, it wasn't guided, and it wasn't something I would recommend to anyone else. There was real risk in it—risk I didn't fully understand at the time. I didn't know what it would do to my body, didn't know how I would react, and didn't know what would come with it.

At that point, though, it wasn't about doing it the right way. It was about doing something, because doing nothing was what had gotten me there in the first place. I couldn't stay there anymore.

Stopping didn't feel like clarity. It didn't feel like confidence. It felt like stepping into something uncertain without knowing what would come next. There wasn't a sense of relief that came with it and no immediate feeling that things were getting better. If anything, it felt exposed, like I had removed something without knowing what was underneath it.

That part wasn't easy. Once I made that decision, I had to sit with everything that came with it. There was no buffer, no automatic system in place, and nothing to fall back on the way I had been before. It forced me into a position where I had to start paying attention again—to what I was feeling, to what was happening, and to what I had been avoiding. It was uncomfortable, but it was real.

It wasn't clean. The drinking didn't just disappear. It didn't stop overnight or because I decided it should. There were still nights where I fell back into it and still moments where it felt easier to return to what I knew instead of pushing forward into something uncertain. That part didn't just switch off. It lingered. It showed up when things got quiet, when things got heavy, and when it felt easier to return to something familiar instead of staying in something that still didn't feel stable.

But something had shifted. Even when I slipped, it didn't feel the same anymore. It didn't feel automatic. It didn't feel like something I could ignore or justify the way I had before. There was awareness there now. There was a recognition of what I was doing, even if I didn't always stop it. That mattered, because things started slowing down. Not completely and not immediately, but enough that it wasn't running everything the way it had before. Enough that it wasn't the default anymore. Enough that there was space between the decision and the action, even if I didn't always use that space the way I wanted to.

For the first time in a while, that space felt important, because inside that space I had a choice. Not a perfect one. Not an easy one. But a real one. That was new. For the first time in a long time, it felt like I had some influence over what happened next. Not full control, not clarity, and not confidence—but influence. Enough to feel like I wasn't just reacting anymore. Enough to feel like maybe I could start shaping something instead of just being carried by it.

It wasn't big, and it wasn't obvious, but it was there. I held onto that. I didn't try to build something perfect out of it, and I didn't try to turn it into a complete plan or solution. I just held onto the fact that it existed—that there was still a part of me capable of making a decision and following through with it, even if it was small, messy, and nowhere close to fixing everything. Because that meant something was still there. Something I hadn't completely lost.

I told myself I could get it under control. Not all at once. Not perfectly. But enough. Enough to keep moving.

Finding Somewhere to Put It

That was the moment I realized I couldn't just sit with it. All of it—the frustration, the anger, and the weight of everything I had been carrying—didn't disappear just because things started to slow down or because I had finally made a decision to change something. If anything, it became more noticeable. Without everything else filling the space, it had nowhere to hide, nowhere to go, and nowhere to settle into anything that would keep it from building. Before, I had ways to bury it. Ways to keep it at a distance. Ways to stay just busy enough and just distracted enough that I didn't have to sit with it long enough for it to fully take shape.

Now there wasn't.

Without those distractions, everything I had been holding onto stayed exactly where it was. The anger didn't go anywhere. The frustration didn't ease up. The thoughts didn't quiet down. They just sat there, constant and present, filling the space that used to belong to something else. The more time I had to sit in that, the clearer it became that I couldn't keep carrying it the way I had been. If it stayed where it was and kept building the way it always had, it was going to take me right back to where I had just come from. I needed to find somewhere to put it—not something that would magically fix it or make it disappear, but somewhere it could go so it wasn't sitting still inside me.

I didn't have a clear plan. I wasn't thinking in terms of recovery, rebuilding, or anything structured like that. I wasn't trying to create a system or follow something that made sense on paper. I just knew I couldn't keep carrying it the way I had been. It had to go somewhere, and the only place that made sense was the gym. Not because I suddenly became disciplined again or decided I was going to rebuild myself from the ground up, but because it was familiar in a way nothing else was. It was the only place where things still felt clear, where expectations didn't shift, and where effort still meant something.

The first time I walked back in, nothing about it had changed. Same equipment. Same layout. Same environment. But the way it felt was different. Quieter. More focused. Like everything outside of it had been cut off just enough that I could finally breathe without something pressing in from every direction. There wasn't a need to think ahead or figure everything out. There wasn't a need to understand anything beyond what was right in front of me. For the first time in a long time, that felt right.

You pick the weight up. You put it down.

There's no confusion in that. No second-guessing, no interpretation, and no questioning what you're supposed to do or how you're supposed to do it. The standard is right there in front of you, and whether you meet it or not comes down to one thing—you. There's no one else to blame, no external factor to point to, and no way to explain it away. You either do it or you don't. That simplicity was something I hadn't had in a long time. Everything else in my life had been uncertain, shifting in ways I couldn't keep up with or control. Effort didn't always match results, and decisions didn't always lead anywhere I could clearly see. But here, it was immediate. Direct. Honest.

That mattered more than I expected it to.

For the first time in a long time, I could feel the connection between what I was doing and what was happening because of it. There was no delay, no interpretation, and no external variable changing the outcome. It was just effort and response, and that gave me something I had been missing for a long time.

Control.

Not the kind I had been convincing myself I had before. Not something dependent on circumstances, other people, or things I couldn't fully understand. This was different. This was something I could feel in real time, something I could trust because it didn't change based on anything other than what I was willing to put into it. I knew exactly where I stood every time I stepped into that gym, and that clarity was something I hadn't had anywhere else.

So I leaned into it.

I put everything into it—the anger, the frustration, and the hate I had for myself. All of it had somewhere to go now. Not in a way that fixed everything overnight or suddenly made life better, but in a way that kept it from sitting still inside me. In a way that gave it direction instead of letting it build without purpose. Every rep became something. Every set became something. Not because it solved anything, but because it moved something, and that movement mattered.

Over time, that started to change things, even if I didn't recognize it right away. There wasn't a moment where everything clicked and no clear point where I could say this is where it started to get better. It was quieter than that. More gradual. It showed up in small ways, in the consistency of showing up, in the fact that I kept going back, and in the way it slowly became something I could rely on when everything else still felt unstable.

It stopped being about simply getting through the day. It became about having something I could step into. Something that didn't lie to me. Something that didn't shift depending on how I felt. Something that didn't require me to pretend I was okay when I wasn't. It was just there, waiting for me to show up and responding the same way every time I did.

That gave me something I hadn't had in a long time.

Ownership.

Even if it was small. Even if it only lasted an hour at a time. Even if it didn't carry over perfectly into everything else. It was still something that belonged to me, something I could build on, and something that didn't depend on anything outside of what I was willing to put into it. It was mine. For the first time in a long time, that felt like enough—not enough to fix everything or make it all make sense, but enough to start building something again without feeling like it would fall apart the second I let go.

Rebuilding Something Different

It wasn't a clean upward path, and it didn't feel like one either. There were days where things seemed to come together in a way that made sense again, moments where I could feel some level of control returning, even if it didn't look the way it used to. It wasn't tied to who I had been before, and it didn't feel as defined or as solid as I thought it would, but it was real enough that I could recognize it. Real enough that I could hold onto it, even if I didn't fully trust it yet. Those moments mattered more than I realized at the time, not because they fixed anything, but because they gave me just enough to keep going without feeling like I was completely stuck.

That feeling never stayed for long. It would show up, sit there just long enough for me to believe in it, and then shift again. Sometimes gradually and sometimes all at once, but always in a way that reminded me how unstable everything still was. There were days where it felt like I was right back where I started, where nothing felt different and where the weight came back in a way that felt just as heavy as before. Not always for the same reasons and not always in the same way, but enough to make everything I thought I had gained feel temporary.

That's where it got hard. It wasn't just about dealing with the weight itself. It was about not trusting the progress either. It was about feeling something start to come together and then questioning whether it was real or just something that would disappear the next time things shifted. It was about trying to move forward without being able to rely on the idea that forward would stay forward.

There were moments where I slipped back into old habits. Not in a dramatic way and not in a way that felt like everything had collapsed, but in ways that were familiar enough that I recognized them immediately. Patterns I had already seen. Reactions I had already had. Ways of coping that I knew didn't lead anywhere different. Even when I could see it happening and even when I knew exactly where it was going, it didn't always stop me from falling back into it.

That part didn't disappear just because I had decided to change. It stayed close. There were days where it felt easier to stop trying altogether, to fall back into what I already knew, even if I knew exactly where it led. Not because I believed it was better, but because it was familiar and because it didn't require me to keep questioning whether anything I was doing was actually working.

That uncertainty was one of the hardest parts. There was no clear feedback and no moment where I could say this is working and trust that it would hold. There wasn't a point where everything leveled out or settled into something predictable. Everything felt temporary, including progress. What felt real one day could feel distant the next, and there wasn't a way to measure it in a way that made sense.

Learning how to keep moving without that certainty and without that reassurance forced me into something I hadn't experienced before. It wasn't confidence. It wasn't clarity. It was simply the decision to keep going.

Not once and not in a way that solved everything, but over and over again. In moments where it felt like it mattered and in moments where it didn't feel like it mattered at all. On days where it felt like I was moving forward and on days where it felt like I was just trying not to lose ground. A lot of the time, that's all it was. Not progress in a way I could clearly see. Just resistance. Just choosing not to go backwards, even when moving forward didn't feel real yet.

That didn't feel like strength. It didn't feel like growth. It didn't feel like anything I would have pointed to and said this is working. But it was still something, and over time that started to matter.

I didn't keep going because I felt ready. I didn't keep going because I believed everything would work out or because I had reached some point where I trusted the process. Most of the time, I didn't trust it at all. I questioned it. I questioned whether any of it was actually doing anything underneath the surface, whether I was changing or just staying in motion long enough to convince myself that I was.

But I kept going anyway.

Because I didn't have another option that I was willing to accept.

I had already seen what the other side looked like. I had already sat in it long enough to understand how it felt when nothing changed, when everything stayed the same no matter what I told myself or what I tried to ignore.

I wasn't going back there. Not because I knew exactly where I was going, but because I knew exactly where I had been. That was enough to keep moving.

It Wasn't Fixed

I needed somewhere for all of it to go—the anger, the frustration, and the weight I had been carrying for so long. The gym gave me part of that. It became my outlet, not because it solved anything or made things easier, but because it gave me somewhere to take everything I didn't know how to process and put it into something real. Somewhere I could push against something that pushed back, something that didn't require me to understand it before I acted on it. I didn't have to explain anything there or sort through it in a way that felt complete. I could just show up and move, and for a while that was enough.

Up until that point, everything had just been sitting inside me, building without direction, without movement, and without anything to absorb it. The gym didn't fix that. It didn't take anything away or make any of it disappear. But it gave it somewhere to land, somewhere to move instead of just staying still. It gave me a place to go when everything started building again, when the weight came back in a way that felt familiar, and when the thoughts started stacking up enough that I could feel myself slipping back toward something I had already decided I wasn't going to return to. It gave me something I could step into that didn't depend on how I felt or what was going on around me. It was just there, waiting for me to show up.

For the first time in a long time, I felt something that wasn't just anger or numbness. It wasn't clarity, peace, or anything I could fully define, but it was different. Subtle enough that I almost missed it at first, but present enough that I couldn't ignore it once I noticed it. It was movement. Not direction in the sense of knowing where I was going and not a plan or a goal I could clearly point to, but simply the feeling that I wasn't sitting in the same place anymore. Something had shifted enough that I wasn't completely stuck, even if I didn't fully understand what that meant yet.

The gym gave me a way to move physically, to take everything that felt internal and make it external, to push against something and feel effort turn into something tangible. It gave me a space where things made sense in a way the rest of my life didn't yet. Over time, though, it became clear that it wasn't enough on its own. As much as I could move it physically and exhaust it for a period of time, it was still there underneath everything else. Still present. Still unanswered. Still something I didn't fully understand.

That's where something else started to shift.

I started leaning into my doctoral work, not because I had some larger vision for it or because I suddenly saw it as a path forward, but because it was the only other place where I could start making sense of what I had gone through. Up until that point, everything had been reaction. Things happened, I felt them, I responded to them, and then I moved on without ever fully understanding what any of it meant. There was no pause, no space to look at it from the outside, and no way to step back and ask why any of it felt the way it did.

Now there was.

Instead of letting that space fill with the same thoughts over and over again, I started using it differently. I started looking at how other veterans handled transition, trying to understand what I had experienced in a way I hadn't been able to before. I wasn't looking for answers at first, and I wasn't trying to fix or solve anything. I was simply trying to understand why it felt the way it did, why it hit the way it did, and why it didn't match what I thought it was supposed to look like.

That disconnect had been sitting there the entire time. The gap between expectation and reality. The difference between what I thought transition would be and what it actually was. The more I looked into it, the more things started to connect. Not in a way that made everything easier and not in a way that suddenly made everything clear, but in a way that gave it context. In a way that made it feel like what I had gone through wasn't random, isolated, or something that only existed in my experience. There were patterns. There were shared experiences. There were things that lined up in a way I hadn't taken the time to see before.

That started to matter.

For the first time, I wasn't just carrying it anymore. I wasn't just sitting in it or reacting to it. I was looking at it, trying to break it down and understand it in a way that gave it shape instead of just weight. Even though that didn't change what had happened, it changed how it felt to hold it. It wasn't just something I was trapped inside anymore. It was something I could examine, something I could step back from just enough to see differently.

Between those two things—the gym and the work—I started finding something I hadn't had in a while. Not in a sudden way and not in a way that felt like everything shifted all at once, but in something quieter that built over time as I kept showing up to both. It wasn't the same kind of purpose I had before. It wasn't something handed to me or defined for me. It wasn't tied to rank, responsibility, or a role with clear expectations. It was something I was building, slowly, without fully knowing what it would become.

It wasn't perfect, and it didn't fix everything. There were still days where things felt heavy, still moments where it felt like nothing had really changed, and still times where I questioned whether any of it was actually making a difference. But it was something I could move toward. Something that didn't disappear the moment things got hard. Something that existed even when everything else still felt uncertain.

That mattered more than I realized at the time.

It meant I wasn't just reacting anymore. I wasn't just trying to survive what I had already been through. I was starting to build something out of it, even if it was small, even if it was slow, and even if it didn't look like much from the outside.

It was still something.

For the first time in a long time, that felt like enough. Not enough to fix everything or make it all make sense, but enough to keep going without feeling like I was going to fall back into the same place I had just come from.

What It Actually Looked Like

I found something again, but it didn't feel the way I thought it would. It didn't show up all at once, and it didn't come with clarity or confidence or any kind of certainty that things were finally moving in the right direction. If anything, it was harder to recognize because it didn't feel like something new. It just felt like something that hadn't completely disappeared, something that had been there the entire time underneath everything else, even when I couldn't see it.

It wasn't about getting back to who I was. That part took longer to understand than I expected it to, because for a while I kept measuring everything against a version of myself that didn't exist the same way anymore. I kept thinking there was a way to return to it, to rebuild it exactly the way it had been, to make everything line up the way it used to. But the more time passed, the clearer it became that there wasn't a way back in that sense. Not because it was gone completely, but because I wasn't the same person stepping into it.

So I stopped trying to go back.

And that didn't feel like relief. It didn't feel like acceptance in the way people describe it. It felt more like letting go of something I didn't fully understand yet, something I had been holding onto because it was familiar, because it gave me a reference point, because it made everything else feel less uncertain. But once I let go of that, I had to look at what was actually still there.

Not everything. Not some complete version of myself that made sense all at once. Just pieces. Small things that hadn't disappeared, even when everything else felt like it had. Ways of thinking, ways of reacting, things I could still step into even if they didn't feel the same. At first, it didn't feel like much. It didn't feel like purpose or direction or anything that I could clearly define. It just felt like something that existed, something that hadn't gone away.

And over time, that started to matter.

Not because it fixed anything, and not because it replaced what was lost, but because it gave me somewhere to move from instead of just something to move away from. And that's a different kind of direction. It's not as clear, not as structured, not as easy to follow, but it's real in a way that doesn't depend on everything being figured out first.

There are still days where it shows up. The anger, the doubt, the weight of everything I did and everything I lost—they don't disappear just because I've made changes or put things in place that help me manage it. They come back in ways that feel familiar, sometimes expected and sometimes not, sometimes in moments where I have space for it and sometimes when I don't.

And when it does, it doesn't feel like something new.

It feels like something I already know.

Something I've sat in before.

Something I've had to move through before.

But it doesn't take everything with it anymore.

It doesn't pull me all the way back into it the way it used to.

There's space now, even if it's small, even if I don't always use it the way I should. Space between what I feel and what I do with it. Space that didn't exist before, or at least not in a way I could recognize or use.

And that space changes things.

Not all at once, and not in a way that makes everything easier, but enough that I'm not stuck in the same place every time it shows up.

There are people sitting in that space right now, in that same place where it feels like nothing is moving and nothing is changing and nothing is going to. Thinking the same things, feeling like this is just what it is now, like there isn't anything past it, like whatever version of them existed before is gone in a way that doesn't come back.

I've been there.

Long enough that it started to feel normal.

Long enough that I stopped questioning whether it could be different.

And that's the part that's hard to explain to someone who hasn't felt it, because from the outside it doesn't always look like anything is wrong. It doesn't always show up in a way that people recognize or respond to. But from the inside, it feels like there's nowhere else to go, like everything just circles back to the same place no matter what you do.

And if you've been there, you understand something most people don't.

You understand what it feels like when everything that defined you is gone, or at least feels like it is. You understand what it feels like to sit in something long enough that it starts to feel permanent, like it's not something you're moving through but something you're going to stay in.

And if you've found even a small way out of that—even for a moment—then you understand something else too.

That it doesn't have to stay that way.

Not all at once.

Not perfectly.

But enough to keep moving.

Rebuilding Trust

I didn't tell her I was trying to change. That wasn't something I planned out or decided in a clear, structured way. It just felt like the only way it could be real, because up until that point words hadn't meant anything. I had said things before, made promises, told her things would be different, and told myself the same thing more times than I could count, but none of it held. Saying it again didn't feel like it would do anything except repeat something that had already lost its weight. If anything, it felt like it would make things worse, because if I said it and didn't follow through, it would become one more thing I couldn't take back and one more reason not to believe me.

So I didn't say anything.

I just started doing what I could in the only way that felt honest, and that meant it had to be quiet. It had to show up in what I did, not in what I said, because that was the only way it was going to mean anything. At first, it didn't look like much. It wasn't some big shift or a clear turning point that anyone could point to and say something is different now. It was small things, things that probably wouldn't stand out to anyone looking from the outside and things that didn't feel like progress in a way I could measure. It was just showing up differently in moments that used to go a different way, being present in ways I hadn't been before, following through on things I would have let slide, and not disappearing into myself the way I had gotten used to doing.

Even that wasn't consistent. There were still days where I slipped, still moments where I fell back into the same habits, and still times where it felt like I was right back where I started. That made it hard to trust, even for me. I didn't expect her to trust it either, because from her side she had already seen this before. Not the exact same version of it and not in the same way, but close enough that it didn't feel new. It felt like something that could disappear the moment things got hard again, something that could fall apart the second I stopped paying attention to it, and something that could fade the same way everything else had before.

I couldn't argue with that, because I hadn't given her a reason to see it differently yet.

There wasn't a moment where she asked what was different, and there wasn't a conversation where I explained what I was trying to do or why I was doing it. It didn't happen like that. If anything, it was quieter than that and more distant in a way that didn't feel cold but cautious. It felt like she was watching, not stepping fully into it and not fully believing it yet, and I could feel that without it needing to be said. I could feel the hesitation and the space between where we were and where we had been, and that part was harder than I expected it to be.

There's a part of you that wants it to be immediate. A part that wants to say I'm trying now, I'm different now, and you can trust this, and have that be enough. There's a part of you that wants the acknowledgment and the recognition that something has changed, that what you're doing is being seen the way you hope it is. But that's not how it works, especially not when trust has already been broken and someone has already had to live through the uncertainty of not knowing which version of you they were going to get.

That doesn't reset just because you decided to change.

I didn't try to force it, and I didn't try to explain it in a way that would make things easier for me. I didn't ask her to believe it before she was ready, because I knew I hadn't earned that yet. I just kept showing up in the same small ways, in the consistent ways, and in the ways that didn't stand out on their own but slowly started building into something harder to ignore.

Time was the part that mattered more than anything else. It wasn't about what I did once, and it wasn't about a good day, a good week, or even a stretch where things felt like they were moving in the right direction. It was about what happened when it didn't feel like that, when things got heavy again, when it would have been easier to fall back into what I already knew, and when it didn't feel like I was making progress at all. Those were the moments that mattered, because those were the same moments where everything had fallen apart before.

Slowly, without a clear point where I could say this is where it changed, things started shifting. It showed up in small ways at first, in how she responded, in how conversations felt, and in how the space between us didn't feel as heavy as it used to. It wasn't trust all at once, and it wasn't something that came back in a way that felt complete or secure, but it was less hesitation, less distance, and less expectation that everything was going to fall apart the moment something went wrong.

Even then, it wasn't something I could take for granted. If anything, it made me more aware of how fragile it still was and how easy it would be to lose it again if I stopped paying attention or slipped back into the same patterns without realizing it. Now I could see what it looked like when trust started to come back, and I knew exactly what it looked like when it disappeared.

There wasn't a moment where everything was fixed. There wasn't a point where I could say we're good now and feel like that was permanent, because it wasn't. It was something that had to be maintained, something that had to be earned over and over again, not just once. It depended on consistency more than anything else, on showing up the same way when things were hard as when they were easy, and on not letting the moments that used to break everything still have that same control.

Over time, that consistency started to matter more than anything I could have said. It stopped being about convincing her anymore. It became about showing her in ways that didn't require explanation, in ways that didn't rely on promises, and in ways that didn't disappear when things got difficult. Somewhere in that, something shifted for me too. I stopped thinking about it as getting back to what we had before, because that version of it didn't exist the same way anymore. What we were building wasn't a return. It was something different, something that came out of everything that had already happened instead of pretending it hadn't.

That took time to accept, because part of me still wanted it to feel the same, to go back to something familiar, and to not carry the weight of everything that had come with it. But that wasn't realistic, and it wasn't honest either. What we were building now was different. Not worse and not better, just different, and in some ways stronger because it wasn't built on assumptions anymore. It wasn't built on things working because they always had. It was built on awareness, on understanding what had happened, and on knowing what it took not to go back there again.

That doesn't mean it's perfect. It doesn't mean there still aren't moments where things feel heavy or where the past shows up in ways that are hard to ignore, because it does. But it's real, and it's something that exists because of what we've both put into it, not because it was always there.

I didn't tell her I was trying to change. I showed her. That's what made the difference.

Why I'm Telling This

That's why I'm writing this. Not as a "woe is me," and not for sympathy. I'm not looking for anyone to feel bad for me or to see this as something that separates me from everyone else. If anything, it's the opposite. I'm writing it because I know what the bottom looks like. I've been there. I've sat in it long enough to understand how it feels when it stops being something you're trying to get out of and starts feeling like something you just live in, something that becomes familiar enough that you stop questioning whether it can change.

I know how easy it is to get stuck there. How easy it is to believe that's just who you are now, that the version of you that existed before all of it is gone in a way that doesn't come back, and what's left is just something you have to carry. Not something you move through and not something that shifts, but something that becomes part of your baseline. Something you learn to function inside of, even if it never really feels right.

That belief is hard to break. Not because it's true, but because it feels true when you're in it. When you've been there long enough and when you've sat in it without anything changing in a way you can recognize, it starts feeling permanent. Like there isn't a version of life that exists outside of it and like there isn't a way forward that doesn't just circle back to the same place.

But it doesn't have to stay that way.

That doesn't mean it fixes itself, and it doesn't mean there's a clean path out or a moment where everything suddenly makes sense again. My road still isn't perfect. I still fight it every day. The anger, the doubt, and the weight of everything I did and everything I lost don't just disappear because I decided to change something. They stay in ways that feel familiar and in ways that don't, showing up when I expect them and when I don't, sometimes quiet and sometimes harder to ignore.

But they don't control everything anymore.

That's the difference.

Not that it's gone and not that it's been resolved, but that it doesn't take everything with it when it shows up. There's space there now, even if it's small and even if I don't always use it the way I should. There's space between what I feel and what I do with it, space that didn't exist before in a way I could recognize.

Over time, that space starts to matter.

I found something again. Not in who I was and not in trying to get back to a version of myself that doesn't exist the same way anymore, but in what was still there when everything else felt like it had fallen away. It didn't feel like purpose at first, and it didn't come with clarity, direction, or anything that made it easy to define. It was simply something that existed, something I could build from instead of something I was trying to return to.

That changed the way I moved forward. Not all at once and not in a way that made everything easier, but enough that I wasn't just reacting anymore. Enough that I could start building something instead of just trying to hold everything together.

Part of that became helping other people. Not because I had everything figured out and not because I had some perfect version of how this is supposed to look, but because I know there are other people sitting in that same place, thinking the same things, and feeling like there's no way out of it. Feeling like what they're experiencing is permanent in a way that doesn't change.

I know what that feels like. I know how real it feels. I know how convincing it is.

If you've been to the bottom, you understand something most people don't. You understand what it feels like when everything that defined you is gone, or at least feels like it is. You understand what it feels like to sit in something long enough that it stops feeling temporary and starts feeling like somewhere you're going to stay.

If you've found even a small way out of that, even for a moment, then you understand something else too.

It doesn't have to stay that way.

6

Almost

Coming Back Without Being Back

What started to change wasn't everything, and it didn't feel like it either. There wasn't a moment where things suddenly clicked or came back into place, no clear point I could look back on and say that's when it all came together. It didn't feel like I had found myself again or figured anything out in a way that gave me confidence. If anything, it felt smaller than that—subtle shifts that didn't seem like much on their own, things that would have been easy to overlook if I hadn't known what it felt like when they weren't there at all.

Even then, it didn't feel like I was "back." That word didn't fit, because "back" implies something familiar, something recognizable, something you step into and immediately know where you stand. But this didn't feel like that. It didn't feel like returning to anything. It felt like stepping into something that looked the same on the outside but didn't feel the same underneath.

I was there again physically, in the same spaces, around the same people, moving through routines that used to feel automatic. Things that had once required no thought now felt intentional. Every interaction, every decision, and every moment carried more weight than it used to, not because anything around me had changed, but because I had. I could feel that difference in everything.

It showed up in the way I carried myself and in the way I approached things that used to feel simple. Showing up when I said I would, following through on things I normally would have let slide, staying present just a little longer than I had the day before even when it felt uncomfortable, and choosing not to escape even when it would have been easier to fall back into what I already knew. None of it felt significant in the moment, but it was different.

Before, those were the exact things I couldn't hold onto. The small decisions, the follow-through, and the consistency were always the first things to go when everything started to fall apart. Now, they were the first things starting to come back, slowly and in pieces.

That's what made it hard to trust at first. It didn't feel solid. It didn't feel like something I could rely on yet. It felt like something that could disappear the same way everything else had before.

What Trust Actually Looks Like

Coming back didn't feel like coming home. Not in the way I thought it would and not in a way that felt familiar. I was there again physically, in the same spaces, around the same people, stepping back into parts of my life that I had once moved through without thinking. The routines were recognizable. The environment hadn't changed. But even though everything around me looked the same, everything underneath it had changed, and I could feel that difference.

It wasn't supposed to feel the same. Too much had happened. Too much had been broken. The idea that I could just show up, decide to do better, and have everything fall back into place wasn't real. It didn't work like that. The damage that had been done didn't disappear just because I was trying to fix it now. It was still there in the space between conversations, in the way people watched, and in the pauses that didn't used to exist. It was there in the moments where something small carried more weight than it should have because of everything that came before it.

I had to face that. Not fix it all at once and not explain it away. Just face it. Because trust doesn't reset just because you decide it should. It doesn't come back because you say the right things or have the right intentions. It comes back slowly, through consistency, through showing up over and over again in a way that matches what you say you're going to do. Even then, it doesn't show up all at once. It builds in small moments, in the times you follow through, in the times you don't fall back, and in the times you choose something different even when no one is watching.

For a while, it feels like nothing is changing. You show up. You do what you're supposed to do. You try to be consistent. But you don't get immediate feedback. You don't get reassurance. You don't get a moment where everything suddenly feels okay again. There's just space, and in that space you're left wondering if it's actually working.

That was one of the hardest parts. I wanted to fix it. I wanted to make it right. I wanted to close the gap between what had happened and where I was trying to go. But I didn't get to rush that. I had to sit in it. I had to accept that the timeline wasn't mine anymore and that the trust I had broken wasn't mine to give back. It was something that had to be rebuilt over time through actions that held up long enough to matter.

That meant I had to earn it back. Not once and not in one moment, but over and over again.

The Weight of What I Did

My wife didn't trust me. Not fully, and she shouldn't have. I had given her every reason not to. Not in one moment and not in one mistake, but over time through the things I did, the things I didn't do, and the ways I showed up when it mattered most. It wasn't something I could point to and isolate. It was a pattern, a buildup, and something that didn't happen all at once but still carried the same weight.

I could see it, not always in what she said, but in how things felt. I could see it in the hesitation that hadn't been there before, in the way certain moments carried more distance than they used to, and in the space between us that I didn't know how to close because I knew I was the one who created it.

That's something I had to sit with. There was no arguing it, no defending it, and no explaining it away. There was only owning it. Owning it didn't mean saying the right things. It didn't mean apologizing in a way that made it easier in the moment. It meant accepting where I actually stood without trying to move it forward before it was ready, even when it didn't feel good and even when it made me question everything about myself.

That's the part no one really prepares you for—the moment where you're no longer trying to prove that you're changing, but instead sitting in the reality of what you've already done. There's no immediate way to fix it and no action that instantly balances it out. There's just time, consistency, and the weight of knowing you're the reason things feel the way they do.

What Showing Up Actually Meant

Showing up didn't look the way I thought it would. It wasn't some big gesture, and it wasn't a moment where everything shifted and people could clearly see that I was different. There wasn't a conversation that fixed it or an action that made everything feel okay again. It was smaller than that, a lot smaller.

Showing up meant being there when I said I would be. It meant following through on things that, before, I would have let slide. It meant doing the things I said I was going to do, even when no one acknowledged it and even when it didn't feel like it was making a difference. Most of the time, it didn't feel like it was. There was no immediate reward, no reassurance that it was working, and no moment where someone stopped and said, okay, I see it now. It was just repetition, doing the same things the right way over and over again without knowing when, or if, it would start to matter.

That was the hardest part. I was used to results. Used to feedback. Used to knowing where I stood based on what I did. But this wasn't like that. This was doing the work without getting anything back right away, without confirmation, without clarity, and just trusting that it would matter eventually even when there was no proof yet.

That meant showing up even on the days I didn't feel like I deserved to. It meant showing up when it felt uncomfortable, when it would have been easier to pull back, avoid the tension, and give myself space instead of stepping into it. It meant being present even when I could feel the distance, when conversations were short, when things didn't feel normal, and when the connection I used to rely on wasn't there the same way anymore.

Showing up wasn't about fixing how things felt in the moment. It was about not making them worse.

It was about proving over time that I could be consistent, that I could be relied on, not because I said I would be, but because I actually was. That doesn't happen in one moment. It happens quietly, in repetition, and in the times no one is paying attention.

Eventually, those moments start to add up. Not all at once and not in a way you can clearly point to, but enough that something begins to shift.

When It Didn't Feel Like It Was Working

There were a lot of days where it didn't feel like any of it was working, not in a dramatic way where something was clearly wrong, but in a quieter way that made it harder to recognize. On the surface, I was doing what I was supposed to do. I was showing up, following through, and making the decisions I knew I needed to make. If someone had looked at it from the outside, it probably would have looked like progress, like things were stabilizing and like I was doing what I needed to do.

Underneath that, though, it didn't feel different yet. It just felt like effort. It felt like I had changed what I was doing on the outside while everything on the inside still felt the same. The same weight was there. The same thoughts were there. The same pull toward everything I had been trying to move away from was still sitting underneath it all. That disconnect started getting to me because I was doing the work. I was showing up. I was trying. Still, there was no clear sign that it was actually changing anything where it mattered.

There was no feedback, no reassurance, and no moment where things suddenly became clear. There was just time and a lot of waiting.

That's the part that makes it hard to keep going. When you're putting in the effort and you don't see the result, when you're trying to trust something that isn't giving you anything back yet, and when the only thing you have to rely on is the belief that it might matter eventually even though there's nothing in front of you proving it.

That's where your mind starts to drift. Not all at once and not in a way that feels obvious, but through small thoughts that show up in between everything else. Questions that don't have clear answers and doubt that doesn't announce itself but stays long enough to be noticed.

What if this isn't doing anything? What if I waited too long? What if I already did too much damage? What if this version of things doesn't even exist anymore?

Those thoughts didn't hit all at once. They showed up quietly in the space between everything else, and that made them harder to deal with because there was nothing immediate to push back against them. There was no clear evidence to prove them wrong and no moment where I could point to something and say this is working. There was only repetition, doing the same things over and over again and hoping that something underneath it was shifting even if I couldn't feel it yet.

That kind of uncertainty wears on you because it would have been easier to go back to what I already knew. Not because it was better, but because it was familiar. Even if it led somewhere I didn't want to go, at least I understood it. At least I didn't have to question whether it was working.

That's what makes staying in it difficult. Not the effort, but the lack of confirmation. The feeling that you're putting everything into something that hasn't shown you anything back yet.

But I had already seen what the other side looked like. I had already lived that version of my life, the one where I stopped trying, where I let things slide, and where I convinced myself it wasn't that bad or that I would deal with it later. I knew exactly where that path led, not because someone told me, but because I had already been there.

That made it real in a way that didn't leave room for negotiation. Even when this didn't feel like it was working, I knew going back wasn't.

So I kept going. Not because I felt confident in it and not because I believed everything would work out, but because I understood what the alternative actually was.

That was enough.

Failing While Trying

There were days where it felt like none of it mattered, not because I wasn't trying, but because it didn't seem like it changed how I was being seen.

I was doing the work. I was showing up, following through, and trying to be consistent. Still, it felt like everything I did was being filtered through who I had already been. No matter what I did in the present, it was still being measured against my past. Every effort and every step forward carried the weight of what came before it.

That's frustrating because part of you wants recognition. Part of you wants someone to acknowledge it, to say they see the effort and that they see you trying to be different. You want some kind of sign that what you're doing is making a difference, that it's not just something you feel, but something that's actually being seen.

But that's not how it works, at least not at first.

The reality is people don't trust what you say. They trust what you consistently show them over time. When trust has been broken, it takes more than a few good days or a handful of right decisions to shift how you're seen. It takes repetition. It takes time. It takes showing up the same way long enough that it stops feeling temporary.

That time feels longer when you're in it, longer than feels fair in the moment, especially when you feel like you're doing everything right now even if you hadn't before. But that's part of it. The timeline doesn't reset just because you decided to change. It carries everything that came before it, and the people around you are responding to that whether you want them to or not.

That was something I had to learn. I had to accept that the work I was putting in wasn't going to be immediately recognized, that the effort didn't erase the past, and that showing up for a few days or even a few weeks didn't undo everything that had already happened. It didn't change how I was seen overnight, and it didn't rebuild what had been broken in a way that could be felt right away.

That didn't mean it wasn't working.

It just meant I wasn't there yet.

What Kept Me Moving

The only thing that kept me going was understanding one simple truth: I had already seen what happens when I stop trying. I had already lived that version of my life, the one where I gave in, where I let things slip, and where I convinced myself it wasn't that bad or that I could manage it later. I knew exactly where that path led, not because someone warned me about it, but because I had already walked it. I had already felt what it did to me, what it did to the people around me, and how quickly things could unravel when I stopped paying attention.

I wasn't going back there.

That didn't make things easier. There were still days where it felt pointless, where the effort didn't seem to matter, and where nothing around me looked different enough to justify the work I was putting in. There were days where it felt like I was doing everything right and still not seeing anything change. Moments where it would have been easier to stop and fall back into what I already knew, even knowing exactly where it would lead.

But I didn't.

Not because I felt strong and not because I had some deep sense of confidence in what I was doing. Most of the time, I didn't. There wasn't a steady feeling pushing me forward or reminding me that it was all going to work out. If anything, there were more questions than answers and more doubt than certainty. Still, I kept going because I understood what the alternative actually was.

It wasn't unknown. It wasn't a question. It was something I had already experienced.

That made it real in a way that didn't leave room for negotiation. I didn't have to guess what would happen if I stopped showing up. I didn't have to imagine where it might lead. I already knew. That knowledge stayed with me, not as motivation and not as something that made it easier, but as something that made it clear.

That was enough to keep me moving.

What Actually Started to Change

At first, nothing about it felt different. I was still showing up, still doing the work, and still making the decisions I knew I needed to make. For a while, it felt exactly the same as everything that came before it—effort without anything coming back, consistency without any clear sign that it was actually doing anything underneath the surface.

If anything, it felt like I was just getting better at going through the motions. That's what made it hard to recognize when something actually started to shift, because it didn't happen in a way that stood out. There wasn't a moment where everything changed and no clear break between before and after. It showed up in things that would have been easy to overlook if I hadn't known what it felt like when they weren't there.

It showed up in the way I responded instead of reacting, in the way I stayed present just a little longer than I used to, and in the way I followed through on something I would have walked away from before. None of it was dramatic. None of it would have stood out to anyone watching from the outside. But it was different.

Before, those moments didn't feel like choices. They felt automatic, like whatever I felt in the moment dictated what I did next without any space in between. If something hit me the wrong way, I reacted. If something felt uncomfortable, I avoided it. If something required more than I wanted to give, I found a way out of it. There wasn't a pause, there wasn't a decision, and there was only reaction.

Now there was space.

Not a lot and not something I always used the right way, but enough to notice. Enough to recognize what was happening before I moved into it. Enough to feel that split second where I could either do what I had always done or choose something different.

That space changed everything.

Not because it made things easier, because it didn't. If anything, it made things harder at first because now I was aware of the choice. I could see the pull toward the old patterns, feel how easy it would be to fall back into them, and still have to decide not to.

That's not comfortable. That's not automatic. That's work.

Over time, though, that space started to feel more familiar. The pull toward old habits didn't disappear, but it didn't have the same control over me anymore. It was still there and I could still feel it, but it didn't dictate what happened next the way it used to.

That was new.

For the first time in a long time, it didn't feel like everything was happening to me without any say in it. It felt like I had a role in it again, even if it was small and even if it didn't look like much yet.

Those small moments started to add up. Not in a way that felt fast and not in a way that made everything easier, but in a way that made it clear something underneath it was shifting. The way I thought, the way I responded, and the way I moved through things that used to control me without question all started to change.

That's when it started to feel different.

Not fixed and not complete, but different enough that I could recognize it. Different enough that I wasn't just trying to survive the day anymore.

I was starting to shape it.

Understanding Accountability

The changes weren't obvious at first. They didn't show up in big moments or clear turning points. They were small and subtle, easy to miss if you weren't paying attention. They were the kind of shifts that don't stand out on their own but start to mean something when you look at them over time. It showed up in conversations that didn't turn into arguments, in moments where I stayed present instead of checking out, and in days where things felt just a little more stable even if I couldn't explain why.

Nothing dramatic, but it was different.

Over time, those moments started to add up. Not all at once and not in a way that felt consistent every day, but enough to notice that something was changing. I wasn't reacting the same way I used to. I wasn't defaulting to the same patterns without thinking. There were moments, small but real, where I made a different choice than I would have before.

That's where accountability started to mean something different.

It wasn't about saying I would do better, and it wasn't about explaining what had happened or trying to justify where I had been. It wasn't something I could talk my way into or promise my way through. It showed up in what I actually did in those moments, choosing to stay in a conversation instead of walking away, choosing to listen instead of shutting down, and choosing to follow through on something I said I would do even when it would have been easier not to.

That's what accountability looked like.

Not words. Not intentions. Decisions repeated enough times to start becoming something real.

Still in It

One of the hardest things I had to accept was this: accountability isn't something you do once.

It's not a decision you make and then move on from. It's not something you check off when you've said the right things or taken a few steps in the right direction. It doesn't work like that. It's something you live every day, in how you show up, in how you respond, in the decisions you make when no one is watching, and in the moments that would have been easy to handle differently before. It's built in the small things, the ones that don't feel significant on their own but end up defining who you are over time.

It doesn’t go away. Not when things get easier. Not when people start to trust you again. Not even when you start to feel more like yourself. It stays because it has to. It’s the only way to make sure you don’t fall back into what you already know you’re capable of becoming. It’s not about punishment or holding onto the past. It’s about awareness, about keeping something in front of you so you don’t drift back without realizing it.

That’s not easy because it forces you to face yourself in a way that doesn’t leave room for anything else. There are no excuses, no deflection, and no version of the story where things look better than they actually are. There is only the truth exactly as it is, whether it feels good or not.

Learning how to live with that, without running from it and without trying to soften it, is part of what keeps you moving forward. Not because it makes things easier, but because it keeps things real. It keeps you honest in a way that doesn’t let you slip back into the same patterns without noticing.

Because you’re not past it.

You’re still in it.

7

Finding Myself

Who I Am Now

I've had to accept who I am now. Not who I was and not some version of me I kept trying to get back to. For a long time, I held onto that idea, that if I just worked hard enough or pushed far enough, I could return to who I used to be. I believed there was a version of me waiting on the other side of all of this unchanged, just buried underneath everything I had been through. Over time, though, I had to face something I didn't want to admit.

That version of me doesn't exist anymore.

I had to stop chasing it.

I had to accept who I am now, someone who broke and someone who isn't fully fixed. Sitting with that wasn't easy at first because it didn't match what I thought I was supposed to be. It didn't match the image I had carried of myself for so long. The more I sat with it, though, the more I realized maybe that isn't something unique to me. Maybe none of us are fully put back together the way we think we're supposed to be. Maybe we don't return to who we were. Maybe we just learn how to carry what we've been through in a way that lets us keep moving forward.

That didn't make it easier.

For a long time, I found myself looking back and comparing my life to people I thought were more deserving. People with longer careers, more accomplishments, and people who had impacted more lives. People who didn't make it back the way I did. That comparison didn't come from clarity. It came from guilt, from trying to make sense of something that didn't feel like it should have worked out the way it did.

That thought sits heavy.

Why them?

Why not me?

There isn't a clean answer for that. There's no explanation that makes it make sense in a way that feels right. Eventually, I had to stop trying to find one because no matter how many times I asked it and no matter how long I sat with it, it didn't change anything. It didn't bring clarity and it didn't make the weight any lighter.

It just kept me stuck.

So I let it go. Not because I understood it and not because it stopped mattering, but because I knew I couldn't keep carrying it the way I had been without letting it define everything that came next.

Accepting What Is

I've had to accept who I am now. Not who I was and not some version of me I kept trying to get back to. For a long time, I held onto the idea that if I just pushed hard enough and stayed disciplined enough, I could return to the person I used to be. I believed there was a version of me still out there unchanged, just waiting for me to find my way back to it. Over time, though, I had to face something I didn't want to admit.

That version of me doesn't exist anymore.

I had to stop chasing it.

I had to accept who I am now, someone who broke and someone who isn't fully fixed. Sitting with that wasn't easy because it didn't match what I thought I was supposed to be. It didn't match the standard I had held myself to for so long. The more I sat with it, though, the more I started to realize maybe that isn't something unique to me. Maybe none of us are fully put back together the way we think we should be. Maybe we don't go back to who we were. Maybe we just learn how to carry what we've been through in a way that lets us keep moving.

That didn't make it easier.

For a long time, I found myself looking back and comparing my life to people I thought were more deserving. People with longer careers, more accomplishments, and people who had changed more lives. People who didn't make it. That comparison didn't come from clarity. It came from weight, from trying to make sense of something that didn't feel like it should have worked out the way it did.

That thought sits heavy.

Why them?

Why not me?

There isn't a clean answer for that. There's no explanation that makes it feel right or settles it in a way that brings peace. Eventually, I had to stop trying to find one because no matter how long I sat with that question, it didn't give me anything back. It didn't bring clarity and it didn't make the weight any lighter.

It just kept me in the same place.

So I let it go. Not because I understood it and not because it stopped mattering, but because I knew I couldn't keep carrying it the way I had been without letting it define everything that came next.

A Different Kind of Purpose

I know my situation isn't the worst. There are people who lost more, people who didn't get the chance to come back from it, and people who never saw hope again or never had the opportunity to figure out what came next. I've had to sit with that, not to minimize what I went through and not to tell myself that it didn't matter, but to understand where I stand in it. I had to recognize that my experience exists alongside theirs, not in competition with it.

I've also had to accept that I'm still here.

That carries weight in a way that's hard to explain because being here doesn't automatically make sense. It doesn't come with an explanation or a reason that ties everything together. It just is. For a long time, I struggled with that, what it meant, why it worked out the way it did, and why I got a chance to move forward when others didn't.

There isn't a clean answer for that.

There's no explanation that makes it feel balanced or fair. The more I tried to find one, the more I realized that wasn't the point. I don't need an answer to understand what it means now, and I don't need to solve it to move forward with it.

What I've come to understand is simpler than that.

It means I still have something to do.

Not in some grand or clearly defined way and not in a way that makes everything that happened feel justified. It doesn't turn any of it into something it wasn't. But being here isn't neutral. It carries weight, perspective, and the responsibility to do something with what I've been through, whether that's showing up differently, being present in a way I wasn't before, or helping someone else see that there's still a way forward.

That matters, even when I don't always feel like it should.

You're Not The Only One

I don't see myself as someone who has it all figured out. I'm not someone who can give you a clean path out of this or hand you a list of steps that suddenly fixes everything. That's not real, and honestly, I don't think it ever was. There isn't a checklist that makes the weight disappear, and there isn't a moment where everything suddenly clicks into place and stays there forever. No one wakes up one day completely healed, completely certain, and completely untouched by what they've been through. That's not how this works.

What I can do is tell the truth about what it looked like for me. The good parts, the bad parts, the parts I'm proud of and the parts I'm not. The moments where I handled things the right way and the moments where I failed the people around me and failed myself. Not because I think my story is somehow unique or more important than anyone else's, but because I know what it feels like to sit inside something you can't explain to the people around you.

I know what it feels like when your own mind stops feeling familiar. I know what it feels like to wake up and not recognize the person you've become. To feel disconnected from people you love while still desperately wanting to connect to them. To carry guilt you can't explain, anger you can't control, and exhaustion that sleep never really fixes. I know what it feels like to sit in silence with thoughts you don't want to say out loud because once they become real, you're scared of what they might mean.

And I know how isolating that becomes.

Because when you're in it, it feels like no one else sees it the way you do. People might see the outside of it. They might see the drinking, the withdrawal, the anger, the distance, or the mistakes. But they don't always see what it feels like underneath all of that. They don't always see how heavy it becomes just trying to exist inside your own head every day. They don't always see how exhausting it is to pretend you're functioning normally while internally everything feels unstable.

That kind of isolation changes you over time. The longer it sits there, the easier it becomes to believe that you're the only one feeling it. The easier it becomes to think maybe something about you is broken in a way that other people wouldn't understand. You start convincing yourself that if people really knew how bad it felt, they would look at you differently. Maybe they would see weakness. Maybe they would see failure. Maybe they would see someone who just couldn't handle it.

So instead, you stay quiet. You carry it by yourself, and eventually that silence starts shaping how you see yourself.

That's part of why I'm writing this. Not because I think my story fixes anything for someone else, but because sometimes the first thing a person needs isn't advice. Sometimes they just need proof that someone else has sat in that same darkness and understands what it actually feels like. Not from the outside looking in, but from inside of it.

Because there's something powerful about realizing you're not crazy, weak, or alone. There's something powerful about hearing another person describe feelings you thought only existed inside of you. It creates space. Maybe only a little at first, but enough to breathe differently for a second. Enough to stop feeling completely isolated inside your own experience.

And that matters more than most people realize.

The first real step usually isn't fixing anything. It's honesty. Not performative honesty. Not saying what people want to hear. Real honesty. The kind where you stop trying to explain everything away and finally admit where you actually are. The kind where you stop minimizing it, stop pretending you still have total control over it, and stop hiding from what's already obvious underneath the surface.

That part is uncomfortable. It forces you to sit with things you would rather avoid. It forces you to look at the damage honestly, to look at the patterns honestly, and to admit that maybe you aren't okay in the way you've been trying to convince yourself you are.

But that honesty matters because nothing changes until you stop running from what's real.

For me, that was one of the hardest parts. Not because I didn't know something was wrong, but because admitting it felt like admitting I had failed. It felt like letting go of the image I had built around myself for so long. The capable one. The dependable one. The one who could handle it. The one who carried things for everyone else without breaking under the weight.

Except I had broken.

And pretending otherwise was destroying me.

That's the part I wish more people understood. You don't have to have everything figured out before you start moving forward. You don't have to suddenly become some perfect version of yourself before things can begin changing. Most of the time, it starts much smaller than that. It starts with honesty. Then it starts with one decision. Then another. Then another. Not dramatic moments. Not life-changing speeches. Small choices repeated consistently enough that they slowly begin shaping something different underneath the surface.

That process is slow, sometimes painfully slow. There are days where it feels like nothing is changing at all. Days where you question whether any of the effort matters. Days where old thoughts and old habits still feel stronger than the progress you're trying to make.

But progress usually doesn't feel dramatic while you're inside of it. A lot of the time, it just feels like continuing, and sometimes continuing is enough.

Because if you're still here, if you're still trying even a little, then the story isn't over yet. Even if you don't fully believe that right now and even if you can't see what comes next yet, you're not the only one sitting in this, and you're not the only one trying to find a way through it.

Who Are You Fighting?

Your situation is yours. No one else has lived it the way you have. No one else has seen it from your perspective or carried it in the exact way you do. The details are different. The experiences are different. The path that brought you here is your own. The things you've seen, the choices you've made, the moments that shaped you, the things you regret, and the things you still don't fully understand all belong to your story in a way no one else can completely step into.

But the feelings are not unique.

The anger. The confusion. The sense of loss. The exhaustion that doesn't fully go away no matter how much you rest. The feeling that something inside of you changed and never fully went back to the way it was before. The question of who you are now and how you're supposed to move forward from something that reshaped you. That part shows up in more people than you think, even if no one is saying it out loud.

Most people aren't saying it out loud.

That's part of what makes it feel so isolating. Everyone learns how to hide it differently. Some people bury themselves in work. Some people disappear into drinking, anger, distractions, or silence. Some people become emotionally distant without even realizing it. Some people convince themselves they're fine because admitting otherwise feels too dangerous. From the outside, a lot of people still look functional while internally they feel like they're hanging on by a thread.

You don't always see the fight people are having with themselves.

That matters because it means what you're feeling isn't something that separates you from everyone else. It's something that connects you, even if you can't see it in the moment. Even if it feels like you're the only one sitting in it. Even if it feels like no one else could possibly understand what's happening inside your head.

You're not alone in that part.

Sometimes just knowing that changes something. Not everything and not all at once, but enough to loosen the grip a little. Enough to create space where before there was only isolation. Enough to realize maybe you aren't failing because you're weak. Maybe you're struggling because you've been carrying something heavy for a long time without knowing how to put it down.

For me, that realization mattered more than I expected it to.

For a long time, I thought the goal was to become who I used to be again. I thought I was fighting to get back to the old version of myself, the one who felt stable, capable, confident, and certain. The version of me that could handle pressure without hesitation, make decisions without doubting myself, and carry responsibility without feeling crushed underneath it. I kept thinking that if I could just push hard enough, work hard enough, and stay disciplined enough, I could force my way back into being that person again.

Eventually, I realized that wasn't really the fight anymore.

The fight wasn't about returning to who I had been before everything happened. The fight was learning how to move forward honestly as the person I had become.

That's a very different thing.

Because eventually you stop fighting the fact that you changed. Eventually you stop wasting energy trying to prove that nothing affected you. Eventually you realize the goal isn't pretending you're untouched. The goal is learning how to carry what happened without letting it destroy everything else around you.

That realization took time.

It took failing more than once. It took hurting people I loved. It took looking at parts of myself I didn't want to admit were there. It took realizing that pretending I was fine wasn't protecting anyone. It was just keeping me trapped in the same cycle over and over again.

That cycle is hard to break because familiar pain still feels familiar, even when it's destroying you.

That's the part people don't always understand. Sometimes people stay in destructive patterns not because they enjoy them, but because they understand them. Even pain becomes predictable after a while, and predictable starts to feel safer than uncertainty. Even when you know it's hurting you, there's a strange comfort in knowing what tomorrow will feel like if you don't change anything.

Change forces you into uncertainty.

And uncertainty is uncomfortable, especially when you've already lost trust in yourself.

That's why the fight usually isn't dramatic. Most of the time it's quiet. It's internal. It's happening in moments nobody else notices. It's deciding not to react the way you normally would. It's staying present in a conversation instead of emotionally checking out. It's choosing not to numb yourself when things start feeling heavy again. It's catching yourself before you spiral into old thinking patterns and making a different choice even when every part of you wants to fall back into what's familiar.

Those moments don't look impressive from the outside.

But they matter.

Because those small moments are what your life eventually becomes built from.

That's something I had to learn slowly. I kept waiting for progress to feel dramatic, for healing to feel obvious, and for there to be some defining moment where I suddenly knew I was okay again. Most of the time, though, progress didn't feel powerful while I was inside of it. Most of the time, it just felt like continuing. Continuing to show up. Continuing to try. Continuing to make better decisions even when I wasn't fully convinced they mattered yet.

A lot of days, it just felt exhausting.

There were days where I questioned whether anything was really changing underneath the surface. Days where old thoughts still showed up. Days where anger still showed up. Days where guilt still showed up. Days where it felt like the version of me I didn't want to become was still sitting right there underneath everything else waiting for a moment of weakness.

Honestly, some days that still happens.

Because this isn't something you beat once and never think about again. You live with it. You learn how to recognize it. You learn how to respond differently to it.

That's what accountability actually becomes over time. Not punishment. Not self-hatred. Awareness. The ability to look honestly at yourself without running from what you see. The ability to recognize where certain choices lead before you fully fall into them again.

That awareness matters because you're still human. You still get tired. You still struggle. You still have moments where old habits feel easier than growth.

Growth is rarely about becoming perfect.

Most of the time, it's about becoming honest enough to stop lying to yourself about where certain paths lead.

Once you truly understand where those paths lead, it changes something. Not all at once, but enough. Enough to pause before making the same mistake again. Enough to choose differently sometimes. Enough to keep moving forward even when you don't fully trust where forward is leading yet.

That's why I ask the question: Who are you fighting?

Because eventually you realize it's not really the world. It's not your job, your circumstances, or even the people around you. A lot of the time, the real fight is internal. It's the version of yourself that wants to shut down. The version that wants to give up. The version that wants to numb everything instead of facing it honestly.

Fighting that version of yourself is exhausting, but it's also where change starts. Not in perfection, and not in pretending you're healed, but in choosing, over and over again, not to let the worst version of your pain make your decisions for you anymore. That choice matters, even when it feels small, even when nobody else sees it, and even when you're still struggling while you make it.

Because every time you choose differently, you create a little more space between who you were becoming and who you still have the chance to be. And sometimes, that small space is where everything starts changing.

A Way Through

I don't have a perfect ending to give you.

I'm still in it. Still figuring things out. Still working through parts of myself that I don't fully understand. There are still moments that don't make sense, still days that feel heavier than they should. There are still times where old thoughts show up, old feelings surface, and things I thought I had moved past suddenly feel closer again. That doesn't go away just because you decide to do better. It doesn't disappear just because you start moving in the right direction.

A lot of people think healing feels clean once it starts. Like once you decide to change, everything slowly becomes easier and more certain from there. That hasn't been my experience. Sometimes progress feels obvious. Sometimes it feels invisible.

Sometimes it feels like growth, and sometimes it just feels like surviving another difficult day without falling backward.

But I know this: there is a way through.

Not easy, not fast, and not the same for everyone. It doesn't follow a straight line, and it doesn't come with guarantees. There isn't a version of it that feels clean or controlled the entire time. There are setbacks. There are moments where you question whether anything is actually changing. There are days where it feels like you're carrying the same weight you started with. But even inside of that, there can still be movement.

I've seen enough of it—in myself and in others—to know that much. Not all at once, and not in a way that suddenly resolves everything, but enough to recognize that it's there. Enough to see people who thought they were completely lost slowly begin reconnecting to themselves again. Enough to watch people who believed they had already destroyed everything still find ways to rebuild relationships, rebuild trust, and rebuild parts of themselves they thought were gone for good.

Most of the time, it starts much smaller than people expect. It doesn't start with having the right answers. It starts with honesty. It starts with being willing to look at where you actually are without turning away from it. Being willing to sit with it, even when it's uncomfortable, even when it doesn't feel like it's leading anywhere yet. Because that part—the part where you stop avoiding it—is what creates the space for anything to change.

That's the part most people try to skip.

We want solutions before honesty. We want certainty before accountability. We want relief before we've fully admitted how heavy things have become. But it doesn't work that way. You can't heal something you refuse to look at directly. You can't move forward honestly while still lying to yourself about where you are.

And that honesty is difficult because it forces you to confront things you've spent a long time trying to outrun. The anger. The guilt. The regret. The disappointment. The exhaustion. The fear that maybe you've already become someone you never wanted to be. That's hard to sit with, but avoiding it doesn't make it disappear. It just gives it more control over you without you realizing it.

For me, that was one of the biggest shifts. The moment I stopped trying to convince myself I was fine and started admitting that I wasn't. The moment I stopped pretending things would somehow correct themselves if I just ignored them long enough. The moment I stopped waiting for things to magically feel normal again and finally accepted that change was going to require something from me. Not perfection. Not immediate transformation. Just honesty.

And then it becomes a decision. Not a perfect one, and not one you make once and never have to think about again. Just an honest one. The kind that doesn't try to dress itself up or make things sound better than they are. A decision to stop pretending it's not there. A decision to stop waiting for it to fix itself. A decision to move, even if you don't fully understand where it's going yet.

Because most of the time, you won't.

Most of the time, you move before you feel ready. Before you feel confident. Before you fully trust yourself again. You move because staying where you are has finally become harder than the fear of changing.

Even then, it's usually not dramatic. It's small decisions repeated over and over again. Getting up when you don't want to. Answering the phone instead of isolating yourself. Having the uncomfortable conversation instead of avoiding it. Showing up when it would be easier not to. Being honest when lying would protect your pride. Choosing not to numb yourself when things start feeling heavy again.

None of those moments feel life changing while they're happening, but they matter because eventually your life starts becoming shaped by those small decisions instead of the destructive patterns you used to fall back into automatically.

That doesn't mean the struggle disappears. It means you slowly stop letting it decide everything for you.

Over time, that changes more than you realize. You start responding differently. Thinking differently. Seeing yourself differently. Not because you suddenly become a different person overnight, but because you slowly stop surrendering every difficult moment to the worst parts of yourself.

That's where the way through actually begins. Not in certainty. Not in motivation. Not in feeling completely healed. But in deciding that even if you don't fully know who you are yet, you're no longer willing to keep becoming the version of yourself that was destroying everything around you.

Eventually, you realize something important: you do not have to be fully healed to start moving forward. You just have to be willing to stop running.

8

It Wasn't Just Me

It Wasn't Just Me

For a long time, I thought what I went through was just me. Not in a dramatic way, and not in a "no one understands me" kind of way. It was quieter than that. More isolating. It felt like something in me had broken, and I didn't have the language to explain it. I couldn't point to it, couldn't define it, and definitely couldn't fix it. So I carried it, assuming that this was just how things were going to be from here on out.

At the time, I didn't know how to separate what I was feeling from who I thought I had become. Everything felt personal. Every struggle felt like evidence that I had failed in some way. Failed to adjust. Failed to move on. Failed to handle something other people seemed capable of handling. And because I didn't hear people talk about those feelings openly, I assumed they either weren't experiencing them, or they were handling them better than I was.

That's what isolation does. It convinces you that your experience is uniquely broken, even when other people are sitting in the exact same silence.

There wasn't a single moment where everything suddenly made sense. No realization that hit all at once and tied everything together. It came slower than that—quieter, almost unnoticed at first. It showed up in pieces. In conversations with other veterans, in passing comments, in stories that sounded a little too familiar.

I'd hear someone describe their transition and catch myself thinking, "Wait… that's exactly how it felt." Not similar. Not close. The same.

Someone talking about feeling disconnected from their family even though they loved them. Someone describing how strange it felt waking up without structure after years of living inside it. Someone explaining how they had a good job, a stable life, and still felt like something inside of them never fully settled after getting out. Someone talking about anger they couldn't explain, or numbness they couldn't shake, or the strange feeling of losing a role that had defined them for so long and not knowing what replaced it afterward.

Every time I heard those things, something in me paused. Because if it really was just me, then how were they saying it too?

That was the first crack in the belief that this was just a personal failure.

At first, I didn't lean into that realization. If I'm being honest, I think part of me didn't want to. Because if it wasn't just me, then that meant something else was going on—something bigger than my own situation. And I didn't know if I was ready to face that yet. It was easier to frame it as an individual problem than to confront the possibility that there was a larger pattern sitting underneath all of it.

But the more I paid attention, the harder it became to ignore.

Different people. Different jobs. Different backgrounds. Different timelines. Some were retired. Some had only recently gotten out. Some looked successful from the outside. Some were struggling openly. But underneath all of those differences, the same themes kept surfacing. The same loss of structure. The same loss of clarity. The same loss of identity. The same feeling of trying to figure out where you fit in a world that doesn't operate the way you were trained to function in.

And it didn't seem to matter how "successful" someone looked on paper. A paycheck didn't automatically fix it. A degree didn't automatically fix it. A new career didn't automatically fix it. People could be doing everything they were supposed to do externally and still feel internally disconnected from themselves and the world around them.

That part mattered because it forced me to realize this wasn't just about employment or stability. It wasn't just about whether veterans could find jobs after the military. It was deeper than that. More internal than that. What people were struggling with wasn't always visible from the outside because a lot of it had nothing to do with external success.

It had to do with identity, purpose, belonging, structure, and meaning. Things that don't show up on a résumé. Things that are hard to explain to people who haven't experienced it.

Once I started recognizing that pattern, I couldn't stop seeing it.

That's when things started to shift for me. Because I realized I wasn't trying to fix a personal failure. I was trying to navigate something that hadn't been clearly understood. Something people were experiencing individually but rarely talking about collectively in a way that captured what it actually felt like from the inside.

That realization didn't solve anything right away. If anything, it complicated things. Because now I had a new question sitting in the background: If this isn't just me, then what is it?

At the time, I wasn't fully in a place where I could chase that question yet. I was still trying to hold my own life together. Trying to rebuild what I had damaged. Trying to figure out how to be present as a husband and a father again. Trying to understand myself enough to stop falling back into the same destructive patterns I had spent years trapped inside of.

But even with all of that going on, the question never went away. It stayed there quietly in the background, persistent and unresolved.

Eventually, I stopped trying to ignore it. I started trying to understand it. Not just for myself, but because I kept seeing the same pattern play out in other people. Good people. Capable people. People who had spent years operating at high levels, carrying responsibility, leading others, surviving difficult environments, and adapting to pressure most civilians would never fully understand.

And then suddenly they were home, struggling in ways that didn't make sense from the outside.

That disconnect stayed with me. Because on paper, a lot of them looked fine. Some had jobs. Some had families. Some had stability. But underneath that, there was still something unresolved. Something they couldn't fully explain. Something they were carrying quietly while trying to continue functioning normally.

That's what pushed me to take a step back and look at it differently—not just as something I was experiencing, but as something worth studying.

That's what led me to my doctoral research. Not because I had everything figured out, but because I didn't. Because I needed to understand why this felt the way it did. Why so many of us experienced the same internal shifts. Why finding a job didn't mean the transition was complete. Why things that used to feel simple suddenly felt heavy. Why so many veterans could appear stable externally while internally feeling disconnected from themselves, from others, and from the lives they were trying to build after service.

What I found wasn't a clean answer or something you could wrap up into a checklist. It was something deeper than that. More human than that.

Veterans weren't just struggling with employment. They were navigating an internal transition—one that involved identity, structure, purpose, meaning, and belonging. Things that don't disappear the moment the uniform comes off. Things that don't automatically rebuild themselves just because someone gets hired somewhere else.

The more I worked through the research, the clearer it became: what I went through wasn't an outlier. It was part of a pattern. A pattern that doesn't get talked about enough, and one that often doesn't get addressed in a way that reflects how deeply internal the experience actually is.

That realization changed the way I looked at everything.

My experience didn't shrink. It expanded. It became part of something larger. Something shared. Something that needed to be understood, not just endured.

And honestly, that changed something inside me too.

Because when you realize you're not the only one carrying something, it changes the way you carry it. The weight doesn't disappear, but it stops feeling isolating in the same way. You stop seeing yourself as uniquely broken and start understanding that maybe what you experienced was part of a larger human response to losing structure, identity, purpose, and belonging all at once.

That perspective matters.

What felt isolating at the time was actually part of a broader pattern experienced by other veterans during transition. The struggle wasn't just external—it was internal, and it was shared. Understanding that shift from "this is just me" to "this is something many of us go through" is the first step in making sense of it.

Mission Debrief

1. Have you ever assumed something you were going through was "just you," only to later realize others experienced it too?
2. What changes when you stop seeing something as a personal failure and start seeing it as part of a larger pattern?
3. Where in your life might understanding replace self-judgment?

9

It Doesn't End When You Leave

Looking Back With a Different Lens

For a long time, I thought what I went through was just mine.

My experience. My failure. My way of handling things—or not handling them. I carried it like it all came back to me: what I did, what I didn't do, where I fell short. And for a while, that made sense, because when you're in it, that's all you can see. You don't see patterns. You don't see systems. You don't see how different parts of your life are interacting with each other. You just feel it—the pressure, the confusion, the loss of control—and you try to manage it the only way you know how.

At the time, everything felt personal. Every setback felt like evidence that I wasn't strong enough. Every bad decision felt like proof that I had failed in some way. I didn't see myself as someone going through a major internal transition. I saw myself as someone who should have been able to handle it better.

That mindset shaped everything. It shaped how I responded to stress. It shaped how hard I was on myself. It shaped the shame I carried every time I struggled with something that used to feel simple. Because in my mind, if I had handled harder things before, then why was I falling apart now? Why did sitting alone in an apartment feel heavier than experiences that should have affected me more? Why did losing structure hit me harder than situations that had actually put my life at risk?

None of that made sense to me then.

But the more distance I got from it, the more I started to realize something: it wasn't just me. Not in the way I thought.

What I went through wasn't random. It wasn't just a series of bad decisions stacked on top of each other. There was a pattern underneath it—something shaping how everything unfolded, something influencing how I responded even when I thought I was acting completely on my own.

I just didn't have the language for it yet.

At the time, I didn't understand what was happening while I was in it. I didn't understand why losing structure hit me the way it did, or why being grounded felt like more than just a career setback. I didn't understand why waking up without purpose slowly turned into feeling disconnected from myself. I didn't understand why sitting in silence felt unbearable some days. And I definitely didn't understand why I couldn't just "push through it" the way I always had before.

Looking back now, I can see it differently.

Not because the experience changed, but because I finally have a way to make sense of it. Not in a way that takes anything away from what I went through, and not in a way that simplifies it into something clean or easy, but in a way that helps explain why it felt the way it did and why I responded the way I did.

It comes down to four things: situation, self, support, and strategies.

At the time, I didn't know any of that. All I knew was that everything felt like it was coming apart, and I didn't know how to stop it. Now I can look back and see that it wasn't just one thing happening in isolation. It was every major part of my life shifting at the same time, without anything stable to hold onto while it was happening.

My situation changed faster than I could process. The structure I relied on disappeared, and nothing replaced it. The role that had defined my day-to-day life, my identity, and my sense of direction was suddenly gone. What used to give me urgency, responsibility, purpose, and clarity no longer existed in the same way. I went from operating inside a system that demanded everything from me to sitting in silence trying to figure out who I was without it.

I wasn't prepared for how hard that shift would hit me.

At the same time, my sense of self started breaking down too. Who I was wasn't just connected to what I did—it was built around it. Being a pilot, being a leader, being someone people depended on wasn't just part of my life. It was the foundation underneath how I saw myself. And when that foundation disappeared, there wasn't much left that felt stable underneath it.

That's what made it feel so disorienting.

I didn't just lose a career path. I lost the framework I had used to understand myself for years. Without that framework, everything else started feeling uncertain too. My confidence. My purpose. My value. Even simple things started feeling heavier because I no longer knew who I was supposed to be inside my own life.

The support around me also became more complicated than I understood at the time. There were people who cared about me. People trying to help. People trying to reach me in ways they knew how. But support only works if you're in a place where you can receive it, and most of the time, I wasn't. Sometimes I pushed people away without realizing I was doing it. Sometimes I isolated myself because it felt easier than admitting how bad things had actually become. Sometimes I convinced myself nobody understood me well enough to help, even when people were trying.

Looking back, I can see how disconnected I had become—not just from other people, but from the idea that I even deserved support in the first place.

And then there were the strategies I used to cope.

At the time, I thought I was managing things. I thought I was finding ways to get through the day, ways to quiet things down enough to keep functioning. But most of the things I leaned on weren't actually helping me move forward. They were helping me avoid what I didn't want to face.

The drinking, the isolation, the distractions, and the emotional distance gave temporary relief, but they also kept me trapped in the same cycle. They helped me escape the weight for a little while without actually changing anything underneath it. Over time, those coping strategies slowly became part of the problem themselves.

At the time, it felt like everything was hitting at once.

And in a way, it was.

Not because I was failing in one specific area, but because all of those areas were shifting simultaneously and I didn't know how to stabilize any of them. My structure was gone. My identity felt unstable. My support systems were strained. And the ways I coped were making things worse instead of better.

That's the part I wish I understood then.

Because maybe I wouldn't have been so hard on myself. Maybe I wouldn't have seen everything through the lens of weakness or personal failure. Maybe I would have recognized it for what it actually was: a transition I wasn't prepared for.

Not just leaving the military, but losing the structure, identity, and systems that had been holding everything together, and trying to rebuild without understanding what was actually happening underneath the surface.

That realization doesn't excuse what happened. It doesn't erase the decisions I made or the impact those decisions had on the people around me. I still own that. I still carry responsibility for the ways I handled things and the damage that came from it.

But it does change how I understand it.

It helps me see that what I went through wasn't just about discipline or willpower. It wasn't simply about trying harder or being mentally tougher. It was about navigating a shift that affected every part of how I lived, thought, functioned, and saw myself.

And I didn't have the tools for it at the time.

So I did what I could with what I had. Some of it helped. A lot of it didn't. But all of it makes more sense now.

And that matters.

Because if you can understand what's actually happening, you can start approaching it differently. Not perfectly, and not all at once, but with awareness instead of confusion. With honesty instead of avoidance. With enough perspective to recognize that what feels like personal failure is sometimes the result of trying to navigate a major internal transition without understanding the weight of what's actually shifting underneath you.

That awareness doesn't solve everything.

But it changes where you start from.

And sometimes, that's where things begin to change.

Mission Debrief

1. What changed around you that you didn't fully process at the time?
Was it sudden, or did it happen gradually without you realizing the impact?

2. How did your sense of identity shift when your role or environment changed?
What part of who you were felt tied to what you did?

3. What support was actually available to you—and were you able to receive it?
If not, what made it hard to accept?

4. What strategies did you rely on to cope?
Did they move you forward... or just help you avoid what you didn't want to face?

5. Are you looking at your situation as a personal failure… or a system of changes happening at once?

What shifts when you see it differently?

10

When Structure Disappears

When Everything Around You Changes (Situation)

I didn't realize how much of my life was built on structure until it was gone.

At the time, it didn't feel like something I depended on. It just felt normal. There was always a place to be, something to prepare for, something that needed my attention. The days had direction, and the decisions had clarity. Even when things were difficult, there was a system around it that made everything make sense. I didn't have to question where I stood or what I was supposed to be doing next, because it was already defined for me.

Looking back now, that structure wasn't just part of my environment. It was what held everything together.

When I was in Afghanistan, the tempo was high, the pressure was constant, and the responsibility didn't turn off. But even in that, there was clarity. You knew your role, you knew your purpose, and you understood what mattered in the moment. There wasn't space to question who you were, because everything around you reinforced it. Even when things started to crack internally, when the panic attacks started and things didn't feel right, I was still operating inside something that gave me direction.

That changed the moment the structure started to disappear.

Being grounded wasn't just losing a position. It was losing direction. The mission stopped, the role shifted, and the expectations became unclear. What replaced it didn't feel like a transition. It felt like a gap. Like something had been removed, and nothing had been put in its place to stabilize it.

WTB made that even more real. On paper, it was support—a place to recover, a system designed to help you through the process. But what it actually felt like was something different. Everything slowed down, but there was nothing to move toward. There was no urgency, no mission, no clear purpose to anchor myself to. Just time, and more space than I knew how to handle.

That's when things started to get loud.

Because when the external structure disappeared, everything internal showed up. The doubt, the confusion, the pressure I had been carrying without fully recognizing it—all of it moved forward at once. There was nothing left to push it aside, nothing left to focus on instead. What had been manageable in the background became unavoidable in the foreground, and I didn't know how to create distance from it anymore.

At the time, I thought I was struggling because something was wrong with me. Because I couldn't adapt fast enough, or because I wasn't handling it the way I thought I should have been able to. I thought if I were stronger, more disciplined, or more mentally tough, I would have adjusted without falling apart the way I did.

But looking back now, it wasn't just me. It was my situation.

Everything that had been holding me steady—structure, mission, clarity, responsibility, and direction—was gone, and nothing had replaced it. That's not a small shift, and it's not something you just adjust to overnight. It's destabilizing, whether you recognize it as that or not.

Because when your environment changes that quickly, and that completely, it doesn't just affect what you do. It affects how you think, how you feel, and how you see yourself. The systems that once kept everything organized internally are no longer there externally, and suddenly you're responsible for creating structure in a space where none exists naturally anymore.

I wasn't prepared for that.

I knew how to operate inside pressure. I knew how to function when expectations were high and responsibility was constant. I knew how to move toward a mission, respond to urgency, and keep going even when things were difficult. But I didn't know how to function in stillness. I didn't know how to exist in a space where nothing was asking something from me anymore.

That was harder than I expected it to be.

Because without structure, time started feeling different. The days stopped having shape to them. There was no rhythm pulling me forward anymore, no external demand forcing me to stay engaged. Without that movement, everything internal became more noticeable. Thoughts that used to stay buried underneath work and responsibility suddenly had space to surface.

And once they surfaced, they stayed.

The doubt, the anger, the confusion, and the feeling that I had lost something I didn't know how to replace all started sitting closer to the surface. At the time, I thought those feelings came out of nowhere. Looking back now, I understand they were already there. Structure had just been keeping them contained long enough for me not to fully notice them.

Once that structure disappeared, there was nowhere left for those things to hide.

That's why it felt like everything was hitting at the same time. Not because it was random, but because it was connected.

I didn't just lose a job. I lost the structure that gave my life direction, the mission that gave my actions meaning, and the clarity that told me where I stood. Without that, I was trying to move forward in a space that didn't feel stable, and I didn't understand why it felt so hard to find my footing again.

That's what transition actually felt like.

Not a step forward, but a loss of footing.

Mission Debrief – Situation

1. What structure in your life used to give you direction—and what happened when it changed or disappeared?
2. When things became quiet, what got louder inside you? Was it doubt, confusion, pressure... or something else?
3. Are you trying to "push through" something that actually requires rebuilding instead?
4. Did your situation change faster than you were able to process it? If so, what part of that are you still catching up to?
5. Are you treating your struggle like a personal failure... or a reaction to a major shift in your environment?

11

Who Am I Without It

The Fight Inside You (Self)

What changed around me was one thing. What happened inside me was something else entirely.

For a long time, I didn't realize how much of who I was was tied to what I did. It wasn't something I thought about, and it wasn't something anyone had to explain to me. It just existed. Being a pilot, being a leader, being part of a unit—it wasn't separate from me. It was how I understood myself, how I measured myself, and how I showed up in the world.

There was no gap between identity and role. They were the same thing.

And when that role started to go away, it didn't leave something behind to fall back on. It created a space I didn't know how to fill. The title was still there for a while, the rank was still there, but it didn't feel connected to anything real anymore. It felt like something I was wearing, not something I was.

That's where the confusion started.

Because on the outside, not everything had changed right away. I was still in. Still showing up. Still around the same people. But internally, it didn't feel the same. The confidence that used to come naturally wasn't there. The clarity I relied on didn't exist in the same way. The certainty I used to move with was gone, and the more I noticed that, the more I started questioning everything about how I was operating.

It wasn't loud at first. It was subtle.

Small moments where I hesitated instead of acting. Times where I second-guessed decisions that used to feel automatic. Conversations where I felt like I was trying to keep up with a version of myself that used to exist, but didn't feel accessible anymore. Those moments didn't stay isolated either. They started building on each other in ways I didn't fully recognize at the time.

Because when you stop trusting how you're showing up, you start pulling back.

Not always in obvious ways, but in ways that create distance. You speak less. You observe more. You stop stepping forward the way you used to—not because you don't care, but because you're not sure if you should anymore. Over time, that hesitation starts feeling like something bigger than just a passing moment.

That's where the internal fight starts. It's not just about what you've lost. It's about who you are without it.

I started questioning things I had never questioned before. Whether I was still capable. Whether I still belonged in the spaces I had once felt confident in. Whether the way I had defined myself still applied, or if I had already proven that it didn't. That kind of questioning doesn't stay contained either. It spreads into everything.

It changes how you carry yourself. It changes how you interact with people. It changes how you interpret the world around you. You start looking for confirmation of what you're already feeling internally, and most of the time, you find it—even when it isn't actually there.

That's what it felt like for me. Like I was slipping, even when nothing around me clearly showed it yet.

The harder I tried to hold onto who I used to be, the more I felt the distance between that version of me and who I was in that moment. It didn't motivate me. It didn't push me forward. It made me feel like I was falling behind some version of myself I could no longer reach.

That's the part no one really explains.

You don't just lose what you do. You lose how you see yourself.

When that happens, it's not just an adjustment. It becomes a fight to figure out what's still there, what's still real, and what you're supposed to build from when everything you used to rely on doesn't feel solid anymore.

I didn't have an answer for that.

All I knew was that I didn't feel like myself anymore.

That feeling followed me everywhere. Into conversations. Into work. Into my marriage. Into the way I thought about myself when nobody else was around. It changed the way I interpreted even small things. A mistake didn't just feel like a mistake anymore. It felt like evidence. A bad day didn't just feel temporary. It felt like confirmation that something inside me had changed in a way I couldn't undo.

That's what made it so heavy.

Eventually, it stops feeling like you're struggling with a situation and starts feeling like the situation is you. Like the confusion, the anger, the disconnection, and the instability aren't things you're experiencing anymore—they're just who you've become.

Once you start believing that, it changes the way you move through everything.

You stop trusting yourself. You stop trusting your decisions. You stop believing your instincts the way you used to. Even simple things become harder because there's no longer a stable version of yourself underneath them that feels reliable. Every decision starts carrying doubt with it. Every interaction feels slightly off. You become hyperaware of yourself in ways that are exhausting because nothing feels natural anymore.

At least, that's how it felt for me.

I kept trying to force myself back into being the person I used to be because I didn't know what else to do. I thought if I could just push harder, stay disciplined, and keep functioning long enough, eventually things would click back into place. Eventually I would feel normal again. Eventually I would feel like myself again.

But that never happened.

Because the harder I chased the old version of myself, the more obvious it became that I wasn't him anymore.

That realization hurt in a way I wasn't prepared for. Not because I thought I had become weak, but because I didn't know who I was supposed to be now. The identity I had relied on for so long no longer felt stable, and nothing had replaced it yet. I was standing in the middle of that gap without knowing how to move through it.

Looking back now, I understand that's why everything felt so personal during that time.

When your identity starts shifting underneath you, every struggle feels connected to your worth. Every setback feels like a statement about who you are. Every failure feels bigger than it actually is because it attaches itself to the fear that maybe you're not the person you thought you were anymore.

That's a difficult thing to carry, especially when you don't have the language to explain it yet.

At the time, I thought I was just failing to adapt.

Now I understand I was trying to rebuild a sense of self while the old one was collapsing underneath me. That process is a lot more painful—and a lot more human—than I ever realized while I was inside of it.

Mission Debrief – Self

1. How much of your identity is tied to what you do–and what happens when that changes?
2. Have you ever felt like you were still "there" on the outside... but not the same on the inside?
3. Where do you notice yourself pulling back instead of stepping forward–and why?
4. Are you trying to hold onto who you used to be... instead of understanding who you are now?
5. What would change if you stopped seeing your struggle as weakness–and started seeing it as identity shift?

12

Learning What You Can Rely On

What Actually Holds You Up (Support)

Support wasn't something I lacked. It was something I didn't fully trust.

Looking back, there were people around me who cared. People who were present, who were trying in their own way to be there for me. My wife, my family, even leadership at times—they didn't disappear. They didn't walk away when things started to shift. The support was there in ways that, from the outside, probably should have been enough.

But that didn't mean I knew how to use it.

At the time, support didn't feel simple. It didn't feel like something I could just reach for when I needed it. It felt complicated, unclear, and in some ways risky. Not because people didn't care, but because I didn't know what would happen if I actually let them see what was going on. There was a part of me that didn't trust how it would be received—a part of me that assumed it would be brushed off, misunderstood, minimized, or turned into something I would have to explain or defend in ways I didn't have the energy for.

Instead of risking that, it felt easier to keep it contained.

So I did.

I filtered what I said. I controlled how much I shared. I gave enough to show I was still there, but not enough to show where I actually was. The more I did that, the easier it became to stay in that pattern, because it created a sense of control. If people didn't fully see it, they couldn't react to it. If they didn't react to it, I didn't have to deal with the vulnerability that came with being fully honest about how unstable things had actually become.

That's how it works sometimes. Not because you don't need support, but because you don't trust what happens if you ask for it.

There was also something else underneath that. I didn't want to put it on them.

My wife already had enough to carry. My family didn't need to carry what I was going through too. In my mind, what I was dealing with didn't feel important enough to justify adding weight to the people I cared about. I told myself it was better to handle it on my own. Better to protect them from it. Better to be the one carrying the weight instead of the one asking for help with it.

When you're inside that mindset, it sounds reasonable. It sounds responsible. It even feels like strength.

But looking back now, I can see that it also created distance.

Because the more you try to become the support for everyone else, the less space you leave for anyone to support you. Over time, that turns into isolation—even when you're surrounded by people who care, even when support technically exists around you.

That's the part I didn't understand then.

I thought I was protecting them, but I was also cutting myself off from the very thing that could have helped me stabilize.

The longer I stayed in that pattern, the harder it became to break. Eventually you stop knowing how to be honest about where you are. You get so used to filtering yourself, minimizing things, and staying emotionally controlled that vulnerability starts feeling unnatural. Even when part of you wants help, another part of you keeps pulling back from it.

That internal conflict is exhausting.

You want people close, but you don't want them to see how bad things feel internally. You want support, but you also feel uncomfortable needing it. You want connection, but you've spent so much time isolating yourself emotionally that even being understood starts feeling unfamiliar.

At least, that's how it felt for me.

There were moments where people tried to reach me and I didn't know how to meet them there. Not because I didn't care, and not because I didn't appreciate it, but because I had spent so much time convincing myself I needed to handle things alone that accepting support started feeling uncomfortable in its own way.

Underneath all of that was pride too.

Not pride in an arrogant sense, but the kind tied to identity. The belief that I was supposed to be capable enough to carry my own weight. That I was supposed to be the stable one. The dependable one. The person other people leaned on, not the person struggling to hold himself together internally.

Admitting I needed help felt like admitting I had failed at being that person.

So instead of leaning into support, I kept trying to manage things myself. I kept believing that if I could just regain enough control internally, eventually I would stabilize without having to fully let people into what was happening.

But that's not what happened.

Trying to carry everything alone didn't make me stronger. It made me more isolated. It made it easier for the drinking, the anger, the emotional distance, and the instability to grow without interruption because there was no real accountability inside isolation. There was nobody fully seeing the extent of what was happening because I had spent so much energy making sure they couldn't.

And the strange part is that even while I was isolating myself emotionally, I still felt frustrated that people didn't fully understand what I was carrying.

Looking back, that contradiction makes sense now.

You can't expect people to fully understand what you never fully allow them to see.

That realization was difficult for me because it forced me to recognize that support is not just about whether people care about you. It's also about whether you allow yourself to be known honestly enough to receive what they're trying to give you.

At the time, I didn't know how to do that.

I didn't know how to separate needing support from feeling weak. I didn't know how to let people into the reality of what I was struggling with without feeling like I was failing in some way. Because of that, I kept trying to survive internally while presenting stability externally.

That only works for so long.

Eventually, the distance between those two versions of yourself becomes exhausting to maintain.

When I look back now, I can see that support was never completely absent from my life. My wife was there. My family was there. People cared more than I allowed myself to fully recognize at the time.

What was missing wasn't support itself.

It was my ability to trust it enough to let it reach me.

Mission Debrief – Support

1. Is support actually unavailable to you... or are you unsure how it will be received if you ask for it?
2. What are you choosing not to say—and who are you trying to protect by keeping it to yourself?
3. Do you trust the people around you to understand you... or are you expecting them to misunderstand you?
4. Are you trying to be the support for others while avoiding being supported yourself?
5. What would change if asking for help didn't feel like adding weight—but sharing it?

13

What Your Strategies Can Do For You

How You Try to Stay Afloat

At the beginning, it wasn't about getting better. It was about not falling apart.

The way I handled things early on wasn't intentional, and it wasn't something I sat down and thought through. It was reaction. Whatever helped me get through the moment, whatever kept things from getting worse right then—that's what I leaned into. Not because it was the right choice, but because it was the only one that felt available at the time.

That's what survival looks like.

It's not clean. It's not structured. It's not something you evaluate while you're in it. You just do what you can to stay afloat, even if you don't fully understand what it's doing to you in the long run.

For me, that showed up in a few different ways. I pulled back. I stopped engaging the way I used to. I controlled what I could and avoided what I couldn't. I leaned on discipline in some areas while completely losing control in others. The drinking became a way to quiet everything I didn't know how to process. Isolation became easier than connection. Avoidance became easier than honesty. Distraction became easier than sitting still long enough to recognize how bad things actually felt internally.

None of it felt like a strategy at the time. It just felt like getting through the day.

And for a while, it worked.

That's the part that makes it hard to recognize, because survival strategies don't fail immediately. They give you just enough relief to keep going, just enough distance from the pain to make it through another day, just enough control to convince yourself that maybe things aren't actually as bad as they feel underneath the surface.

That's what makes them dangerous.

When something helps you survive emotionally in the short term, you stop questioning what it's costing you in the long term. You focus on the relief, not the damage. You focus on getting through the moment, not where the pattern is leading you over time.

That's where I was for a long time.

The drinking quieted things down enough that I didn't have to sit with everything all at once. Pulling away emotionally protected me from conversations I didn't know how to have. Staying distracted gave me something to focus on besides what was happening internally. Even the anger served a purpose in its own way, because anger feels more manageable than helplessness. It feels active. Directed. Easier to carry than confusion or grief.

At the time, I didn't understand any of that consciously. I just knew those things helped me make it through the day without completely collapsing under the weight of everything I was carrying.

But eventually, survival starts changing shape.

The same things that helped you stay afloat start weighing you down instead. What once gave you relief starts creating more pressure. What once helped you avoid the problem starts becoming part of it. The patterns that once felt protective slowly become destructive, and by the time you fully recognize it, they've already worked their way into your life, your relationships, and the way you function.

That's the hard part about unhealthy coping.

It doesn't usually feel destructive in the beginning. It feels necessary.

That's why people stay in it longer than they should, because the behavior itself isn't random. It's attached to relief. It's attached to survival. It's attached to the temporary feeling that maybe you can breathe for a second without everything crashing into you all at once.

But temporary relief is not the same thing as healing.

I didn't understand that then. I thought if I could just manage the pressure enough to function, eventually things would settle on their own. Eventually the weight would pass. Eventually I would feel normal again without having to fully confront what was happening underneath everything else.

That's not what happened.

Instead, the gap kept growing between how I looked externally and how unstable things felt internally. I was surviving, but I wasn't rebuilding. I was avoiding collapse, but I wasn't actually moving forward. Everything became focused on managing symptoms instead of addressing what was underneath them.

Eventually, you reach a point where what you've been doing isn't enough anymore.

You either adapt, or you don't.

And if you don't, the road still leads somewhere. It just takes longer to get there.

For some people, that shift happens gradually. They start recognizing what isn't working before everything completely falls apart. They begin adjusting the way they cope. They start rebuilding structure. They learn healthier ways to process what they're carrying before the damage spreads too far into the rest of their life.

For others, it takes hitting the bottom. It takes reaching a point where there's no way left to ignore it, no way left to justify it, and no way left to pretend the patterns aren't costing something real anymore.

I've been on that side of it.

The truth is, both paths eventually lead to the same realization: you have to change what you're doing. The only difference is how long you stay inside what isn't working before you finally do.

That's when strategies start shifting.

They stop being about survival and start becoming about rebuilding. You begin looking for things that don't just numb the weight temporarily, but actually help you carry it differently. You start replacing avoidance with awareness, control with consistency, and reaction with intention.

That doesn't happen all at once, and it doesn't happen perfectly either.

There were still days where I slipped into old habits mentally. Still days where avoidance felt easier. Still moments where I wanted relief more than growth. But over time, the goal started changing. I wasn't just trying to escape what I felt anymore. I was trying to understand it well enough that it stopped controlling every decision I made.

That shift matters.

Eventually, rebuilding requires different tools than survival does.

Survival is about making it through the moment. Rebuilding is about creating a life you can actually stay present inside of. Those are not the same thing.

For the first time in a long time, I slowly started recognizing that I didn't just want relief anymore. I wanted stability. I wanted honesty. I wanted connection. I wanted to feel present inside my own life again instead of constantly trying to escape parts of it.

That's when things actually started changing.

Not because everything suddenly became easier, but because my strategies finally started moving me somewhere instead of just helping me avoid where I already was.

Because eventually, surviving is not enough anymore.

Eventually, you want to move forward too.

Mission Debrief – Strategies

1. What are you doing right now that helps you get through the day—but might not be helping you move forward?
2. Are your current strategies built around avoiding the problem… or understanding it?
3. Have you reached a point where what used to work… doesn't anymore?
4. Are you adapting your approach—or staying in what's familiar because it feels safer?
5. How long are you willing to stay in something that isn't working before you decide to change it?

14

How It Ties Together

When Everything Hits at Once (Interaction of the 4 S's)

At the time, it felt like everything was happening at once.

The situation changed. The structure was gone. The clarity I relied on disappeared faster than I could process it. At the same time, who I was started to feel unstable. The confidence wasn't there, the identity didn't feel solid, and I didn't know how to define myself without what I used to do. Support was there, but it didn't always land. Not because people didn't care, but because I didn't trust it or didn't know how to receive it. The strategies I leaned on, the things that helped me survive early on, eventually stopped working the way I needed them to.

It all stacked, and when it stacks like that, it doesn't feel like separate problems. It feels like collapse.

That's what I didn't understand then. I thought I was dealing with one thing at a time. I thought if I could fix one area, get back to work, get control of my habits, or get my head right, everything else would fall into place. But none of it exists on its own. Your situation affects how you see yourself. How you see yourself affects how you accept support. Whether or not you accept support shapes the strategies you use to cope, and those strategies either stabilize you or push you further into it.

It's all connected.

When all of it shifts at the same time, it creates a cycle—one that doesn't just happen once, but repeats in ways that aren't always obvious while you're in it. One part starts affecting the others, and eventually everything feeds into itself. The worse things felt internally, the more I pulled away from support. The more isolated I became, the more I relied on unhealthy ways of coping. The more I relied on those strategies, the harder it became to stabilize my life or feel connected to myself again.

At the time, I couldn't see the pattern. I just knew I felt stuck.

That's the part that doesn't get talked about enough. For veterans, this often isn't something you move through once and leave behind. It's not a clean transition where you reach the other side and everything suddenly settles into place. It continues, even after things improve, even after you rebuild parts of your life, and even after you start feeling more stable again.

There are still moments where it comes back. Moments where something shifts externally and triggers something internally. Moments where identity feels unclear again, where support feels distant again, or where the strategies you've been using don't feel as effective as they once did. Sometimes all it takes is a change in environment, a major life event, or even a moment of stillness to bring parts of it back to the surface.

That doesn't mean you've failed. It means you're still human.

The cycle doesn't completely disappear. It evolves.

That's where my understanding of all of this started changing. Over time, I stopped trying to "finish" the process. I stopped searching for some final point where everything would feel resolved, where nothing from the past carried weight anymore, or where I would finally feel completely healed and fully back to who I used to be.

That point doesn't exist.

What does exist is movement. You get better at recognizing what's happening while it's happening. You get better at seeing the patterns before they fully pull you under. You learn how to stabilize yourself instead of waiting for everything around you to feel stable first. You stop expecting perfection and start focusing on awareness, consistency, and honesty instead.

That shift mattered more than I realized at the time.

One of the biggest changes for me was understanding where support actually comes from. For a lot of veterans, support doesn't always come from where you expect it to. It doesn't always come through formal systems, structured conversations, or people trying to help in obvious ways. Sometimes support comes from rebuilding who you are. Sometimes it comes from creating something new to stand on after the old identity no longer feels stable enough to carry everything by itself.

That's where purpose started becoming important again for me.

Not purpose tied to rank, position, or the role I used to have, but something different than that. Something that existed outside the structure I had lost. Helping other veterans. Understanding what transition actually does to people internally. Turning my experience into something that could maybe help someone else recognize they weren't alone in theirs.

That became an anchor. It gave direction when things felt unclear. It created stability when other parts of life felt like they were shifting again. It became something I could return to, even during moments where I still felt the weight of everything I had been through.

That's what started feeling different.

Not because everything was fixed, but because I was no longer waiting for life to become perfect before I allowed myself to move forward inside it.

But even that isn't final.

No matter how far you move forward, there's still a part of you that remembers who you were, what that identity meant, and what it gave you. There are still moments where you feel the absence of it, even if you've built something meaningful in its place.

That doesn't go away, and honestly, I don't think it's supposed to. There will always be a part of you that remembers who you were, what that identity meant, and what it gave you. Those experiences shaped you in ways that don't simply disappear because time passes or life changes.

But this isn't about replacing who you were. It's about learning how to carry that version of yourself without letting it keep you trapped there. It's about accepting that your past will always be part of you while still allowing yourself to keep building something beyond it.

That's the difference.

You don't move on.

You move forward.

Mission Debrief – The Cycle

1. Are you expecting your transition to "end"... or are you learning how to navigate it as it evolves?
2. What happens in your life when your environment shifts—do old patterns start to show up again?
3. Where are you currently finding your sense of stability—from people, from structure, or from purpose?
4. Are you trying to replace who you were... or learn how to carry that identity forward in a different way?
5. What would change if you stopped trying to "arrive"... and focused on learning how to adapt?

15

Understanding the Way Forward

Accepting What Doesn't Come Back

One of the hardest things to accept was this: what I was couldn't be all of who I am now.

For a long time, I kept trying to carry my identity forward in the same form it had always existed in. I held onto it like something I could preserve, like if I stayed close enough to it, I wouldn't lose it completely. Being a pilot, being in that environment, being part of something that carried real weight—that wasn't just what I did. It was how I understood myself, how I measured myself, and how I made sense of where I fit in the world. When that ended, I didn't just lose the role. I lost the version of me that existed inside of it.

That's the part that doesn't get talked about enough. It's not just that things change. It's that some parts of your life don't transfer the way you expect them to. They don't show up the same way in a different environment, and no matter how hard you try, you can't recreate what they felt like. You can remember it. You can miss it. You can carry pieces of it with you. But you can't fully live inside it anymore.

That took time to accept.

Part of me kept trying to go back, even when I knew I couldn't. Not physically, but mentally. I compared everything to what it used to feel like: the clarity, the purpose, and the weight behind what I was doing. There was something about that life that felt bigger than me, something that gave direction without needing to question it. The mission existed. The responsibility existed. The meaning was already there before you even woke up in the morning.

Nothing outside of that felt the same to me for a long time. Not work, not routine, and not normal life. Nothing carried the same intensity or the same sense of immediate purpose. When you've spent years operating in an environment where everything matters at that level, it becomes difficult to reconnect with things that feel quieter by comparison.

That's where purpose started feeling unclear.

When you've lived inside a world where the stakes are real and immediate, normal life can feel strangely disconnected at first. It's hard to look at ordinary routines and feel the same sense of meaning you once attached to your role. It's hard to feel grounded in things that don't carry the same urgency or demand the same version of you that the military once did.

For a while, I kept searching for something that would recreate that feeling. Something that would bring back the same clarity. Something that would make me feel aligned again in the way I once had.

But that's not how it works.

Purpose doesn't come back in the same form.

That was the shift I had to learn how to make. Instead of asking myself how to get the old version back, I had to start asking a different question: where does purpose exist now? Because it was still there. It just didn't look the way I expected it to.

It showed up in quieter places. In my family. In being present in ways I hadn't been before. In the responsibilities I had overlooked when I was still chasing the version of myself I used to be. It showed up in conversations, in consistency, and in learning how to be there emotionally instead of just physically. It showed up in helping other veterans make sense of things I once thought I was carrying alone.

None of that looked the same as the life I had before.

But it was real.

And the more I leaned into that, the more I started understanding that purpose wasn't something I had lost completely. It was something I had to redefine. Not replace, not erase, but rebuild in a way that fit the life I was actually living now instead of the one I kept trying to mentally return to.

That didn't mean I stopped missing who I was. It didn't mean I stopped recognizing what that time in my life meant to me. There are still parts of that identity that I carry proudly, and there are still moments where I feel the weight of what it used to be. There are still days where I miss the clarity of it, the structure of it, and the certainty that came with knowing exactly who you were inside that world.

That doesn't go away, and honestly, I don't think it's supposed to. The military was part of me. It shaped me in ways that will always exist. There are lessons, values, and experiences from that life that will stay with me for the rest of my life. That version of me mattered. It still matters.

But eventually I had to accept that if I kept trying to force my entire identity to stay frozen inside that version of my life, I would never fully step into the one I still had in front of me.

That realization was painful at first. Letting go of the idea of returning to who I was felt like losing something all over again. It felt final in a way I didn't want to accept. It forced me to confront the reality that some chapters of life don't reopen the way we wish they would, no matter how badly we want to return to them.

But over time, I started realizing something important.

Moving forward didn't require me to abandon who I had been. It required me to stop believing that version of me was the only one worth being.

That changed the way I looked at myself. I stopped treating my life like it had peaked in the past. I stopped viewing everything after the military as something lesser simply because it was different. I stopped measuring every new experience against an old standard that nothing else could realistically recreate.

Slowly, that created space for something new. Not a replacement and not a copy of what I had before, but something different. Something quieter, but more grounded. Something built less around performance and identity, and more around presence, honesty, and connection.

That's what finally started changing things for me.

Not the loss of the old identity, but the acceptance that my life still had room to grow beyond it.

Mission Debrief – Purpose

1. Are you trying to recreate who you were... or understand who you are becoming?
2. Where are you currently looking for purpose—and is it based on what you lost or what's in front of you now?
3. Who or what gives your life meaning today? Family? Spouse? Community? A new role?
4. Are you overlooking quieter forms of purpose because they don't feel as intense as what you've experienced before?
5. What would it look like to build purpose around what matters now—not what used to define you?

16

The Change of Purpose

Purpose Doesn't Feel the Same

One of the hardest things to come to terms with was this: purpose doesn't feel the same anymore. For a long time, I thought something was missing because I kept comparing everything in front of me to what I had experienced before—the urgency, the clarity, and the weight behind every decision. There was something about operating in a life-or-death environment that made everything feel immediate, like what you were doing mattered in a way that didn't need to be questioned. The mission existed. The stakes were real. The responsibility was clear. You woke up already knowing why what you were doing mattered, and over time that kind of environment changes the way you measure meaning itself.

When that was gone, everything else felt smaller to me. It didn't carry the same intensity, didn't demand the same level of focus, and didn't feel like it held the same kind of value. For a while, I took that as a sign that something was wrong—that I had lost something I couldn't replace and that normal life simply couldn't compete with what I had already experienced. Looking back now, I can see that I wasn't actually struggling because purpose was gone. I was struggling because I was still measuring purpose by the standards of the life I had before. I expected meaning to show up through urgency, pressure, and immediate consequences because that was the version of purpose I had spent years learning to recognize.

But purpose doesn't always arrive that way, and it doesn't always need to. That was difficult for me to accept because intensity and meaning had become connected in my mind. If something didn't feel urgent, I assumed it wasn't as important. If it didn't carry pressure or high stakes, I struggled to recognize the value in it. I had spent so long operating in environments where everything demanded immediate action that I didn't really know how to appreciate slower forms of purpose anymore. I didn't understand that something could matter deeply without demanding adrenaline, sacrifice, or constant pressure to survive.

Over time, though, I started realizing that slower doesn't mean smaller. It just means different. When one version of purpose disappears, another version becomes possible. You're no longer operating in a space defined by life or death. You're operating in a space where you can create something more sustainable, more intentional, and more connected to the people directly in front of you. That was the shift I had to learn how to make. Purpose was no longer built around urgency or intensity. It started becoming built around presence, consistency, and the ability to contribute to something that lasted longer than a single moment.

At first, that difference felt empty instead of peaceful. I kept searching for something that would recreate the same feeling I once had because I didn't yet understand that purpose after transition was never going to arrive in the same form it once did. I was still looking for intensity when life was trying to teach me stability. I was still looking for external pressure when what I actually needed was connection. Purpose after transition often grows quietly, and that was something I completely missed in the beginning because I was waiting for it to announce itself the way it used to.

Instead, it started showing up in repetition, consistency, relationships, and in building instead of reacting. It showed up in being present long enough for something meaningful to develop over time instead of appearing instantly through urgency and pressure. For a long time, showing up for my family didn't "feel" as significant as the environments I had operated in before, even though it mattered more than I realized. Building stability didn't feel exciting. Being emotionally available didn't create adrenaline. Creating consistency in everyday life didn't feel dramatic enough to register as purpose in the way I was used to defining it.

But eventually I started understanding something important: just because something is quieter doesn't mean it carries less weight. In some ways, it carries more. The purpose now wasn't about reacting to chaos or surviving intense moments. It was about creating something stable enough to last beyond them. That realization changed the way I started seeing my life because I began recognizing meaning in places I had overlooked before. I found it in showing up for my kids, in being present with my wife in ways I hadn't fully understood before, in helping other veterans navigate things I once thought I was carrying alone, and in building consistency instead of constantly living in reaction to pressure.

Those things didn't feel like purpose at first because they didn't feel intense, but they were real in a way I hadn't understood yet. Instead of reacting to something that demanded immediate action, I was creating something that mattered over time. Something that didn't rely on urgency, but on consistency. Something that didn't disappear when the moment ended, but stayed. That's where purpose slowly started feeling real again—not because it replaced what I had before, but because it gave me something new to build.

That doesn't mean I don't miss what it used to feel like. There are still moments where I think about the clarity, the responsibility, and the weight of what I was doing, and I feel the difference. There are still parts of me that miss the intensity of that life and the certainty that came with it. That part doesn't go away, and honestly, I don't think it's supposed to. This isn't about forgetting that version of purpose or pretending it didn't matter. It's about understanding that purpose evolves, and that the opportunity to build meaning didn't end when one chapter of life closed. It simply changed shape, and learning how to recognize that new shape was part of learning how to move forward again.

Mission Debrief – Purpose Reframed

1. Are you judging your current purpose by the intensity of your past—or the meaning it holds now?
2. Where in your life are you creating hope or joy for someone else?
3. Are you overlooking meaningful roles because they don't feel as urgent or intense as what you've experienced before?
4. What would it look like to build purpose around consistency instead of intensity?
5. Who in your life benefits from you showing up—not in crisis, but in presence?

17

Creation

Rebuilding Without a Blueprint

One of the hardest things to accept was that the structure I relied on wasn't coming back. Not in the way I knew it, and not in a way I could just step back into. For a long time, I held onto the idea that I just needed to find the right path, the right role, or the right environment, and everything would fall back into place—that if I could recreate enough of what I had before, I would feel like myself again.

But that never happened.

The more I chased that idea, the more I realized the structure I had before wasn't something I could recover. It belonged to a specific chapter of my life, a specific environment, and a specific version of me that no longer existed in the same way. I could remember it. I could miss it. I could wish parts of it still existed. But I couldn't rebuild my life by trying to force myself back into something that only made sense inside the world I had already left behind.

That realization was difficult because the structure I had before gave me direction without requiring me to constantly question myself. It told me where to be, what mattered, and how to measure myself. It removed uncertainty, and in a lot of ways, it removed the burden of having to figure things out alone. The expectations already existed before I even stepped into the day, and my role inside that structure gave me clarity about who I was and what I was responsible for.

Without it, everything felt open in a way that was uncomfortable. There were too many directions, too many choices, and no clear system telling me what mattered most anymore. When you spend years operating inside something that gives you that level of clarity, freedom doesn't automatically feel empowering. Sometimes it feels unstable. Sometimes it feels like standing in an open space without knowing where you're supposed to move next.

That's where I stayed stuck for a while. I kept waiting for something external to recreate the feeling of stability I used to have instead of realizing the old structure wasn't coming back in the same form. I thought I needed another system to step into, another role that would immediately restore the same sense of direction and certainty I had before.

But over time, I started understanding something differently.

The structure being gone wasn't just something I lost. It was also something I gained control over.

That's the part I didn't see at first because the structure I had before worked, but it wasn't built around me as an individual. It was built around the mission. It was built around the unit. It was built around something larger than any one person, and my role was to function inside it the way I had been trained to.

Now that structure was gone, and what replaced it wasn't handed to me. I had to build it myself.

That changed everything because now structure wasn't something I automatically followed anymore. It became something I intentionally created. At first, that didn't feel natural. I questioned it constantly. I second-guessed whether the routines, habits, and systems I was trying to put in place actually mattered because there was nothing external measuring them the way military life once had.

There was no immediate feedback, no clear standard, and no certainty that I was doing it right. That uncertainty was uncomfortable because I had spent so much of my life operating inside systems where expectations were already defined. Now I had to figure out what stability looked like for me personally, not just professionally. I had to decide what mattered enough to build my life around without relying on urgency, rank, or external structure to define it for me.

That took time.

But slowly, things started settling into place in a different way. I began taking pieces of what I had learned before—discipline, consistency, accountability, and routine—and applying them in ways that actually fit the life I was living now instead of the life I kept trying to mentally return to. The structure stopped being about performance alone and started becoming about stability. It stopped being about proving something externally and started becoming about creating something internally that could actually support me long term.

That shift mattered more than I realized. For the first time, the systems I was building weren't just demanding something from me. They were supporting me too. They gave me space to recognize what was happening internally instead of constantly pushing past it. They helped me understand how I was responding to stress, what patterns pulled me backward, and what actually helped me move forward in a sustainable way.

That created a different kind of control. Not the rigid control I associated with military structure, but something more balanced. Something that allowed me to stay accountable without losing awareness of myself in the process. Something that helped me recognize when I was struggling instead of forcing myself to ignore it until everything collapsed again.

That's where the shift really started happening.

I stopped reacting to my situation and slowly started shaping it instead.

That didn't mean everything suddenly became easy. There were still days where things felt uncertain, where the structure I was building didn't feel solid, and where I questioned whether I was doing any of it the right way. There were still moments where old habits felt easier than staying consistent with the life I was trying to build.

But even during those moments, something had changed.

I wasn't waiting for someone else to create stability for me anymore. I wasn't waiting for the perfect environment, the perfect role, or the perfect situation to finally make me feel grounded again. I was building that foundation myself.

And for the first time in a long time, that gave me something I hadn't realized I lost along the way.

A fighting chance.

Mission Debrief – Structure & Control

1. Are you waiting for structure to return... or are you willing to build it yourself?
2. What parts of your past structure still serve you—and how can you adapt them to your life now?
3. Do you see freedom as opportunity... or instability? Why?
4. What systems or habits are you creating that actually support you—not just demand from you?
5. Where in your life can you shift from reacting... to shaping what comes next?

18

What Does It Do For Me Now?

The Weight That Doesn't Leave

Some parts of this don't go away, and they're not supposed to. Not everyone feels it the same way either. Some people are tied to that identity more deeply than others. Some of you may have already started letting pieces of it go, while others still feel like that version of yourself is the only version that ever fully made sense. Wherever you fall in that, it doesn't make you right or wrong. It just means that part of your life mattered to you in a way that left a mark.

It's okay to miss that person. It's okay to miss the way you felt when things were clear, when your role made sense, and when the structure around you gave you a kind of confidence and certainty that didn't need to be questioned. Missing that doesn't mean you're failing to move forward, and it doesn't mean you're stuck in the past. It means you experienced something that shaped you deeply enough to leave an imprint that doesn't simply disappear because time passed. Honestly, you'd be a fool not to miss it, because that part of your life carried something most people will never fully understand. It gave you a sense of purpose, connection, and meaning that wasn't surface level. It wasn't casual, and it wasn't built under normal circumstances. It was built under pressure, in environments where people relied on each other completely and where what you did actually mattered in immediate and visible ways.

That kind of connection doesn't just disappear. There's a saying we use—miss the monkeys, not the circus—and that's exactly what a lot of this becomes over time. You don't always miss the system. You don't always miss every part of the organization or everything that came with it. But you miss the people. You miss the ones you served with, the ones who understood you without needing things explained, and the ones who existed beside you during experiences that most people outside that world will never fully relate to. Relationships built in those environments carry a different kind of weight because they were formed under pressure, where trust wasn't theoretical and where people saw sides of each other that rarely come out anywhere else.

For some people, there's something even heavier underneath all of that: the people who didn't make it. The ones who don't get to figure this part out. The ones who don't get to move forward, even when moving forward feels confusing or painful. The ones whose stories stopped while yours kept going. When you sit with that long enough, it can turn into guilt. You start asking questions that don't have answers. Why them? Why not me? And if you hold onto those questions the wrong way, they can keep you trapped in something that never fully resolves. You can spend years replaying it in your head, trying to make sense of something that simply doesn't make sense in a way that feels fair.

I've had to learn that there are some questions in life that don't give you closure. But I've also learned there's another way to carry those memories. Because what you had with those people—what you saw, what you experienced together, the way you knew them—is something most of the world will never fully understand. You got to see people stripped down to who they really were underneath everything else. You saw courage, fear, sacrifice, humor, loyalty, and humanity in environments where none of it could be faked for very long. Those experiences don't disappear once the environment is gone. They become part of you in ways that continue shaping how you see the world long after those moments are over.

That's the part you don't lose. Not the title or the role, but the people, the lessons, and the perspective that came with those experiences. Over time, I've started understanding that carrying those things forward doesn't mean staying trapped in the past. It means allowing those experiences to continue shaping who you are without letting them prevent you from becoming something more than only that version of yourself. This isn't about forgetting where you came from. It's about learning how to carry it in a way that strengthens you instead of holding you down. You don't move on from it. You carry it forward.

Mission Debrief – The Weight

1. What part of who you were do you still miss—and what did it give you that mattered?
2. Are you trying to get rid of that part of your life... or learn how to carry it differently?
3. Who do you "miss"—the system, or the people you shared it with?
4. Are you holding onto guilt in a way that holds you back—or can it be reshaped into something that strengthens you?
5. What memories or relationships from that time are still shaping how you live today?

19

Power In Committing

Learning How to Carry It

Some parts of this don't go away, and they're not supposed to. Not everyone feels it the same way either. Some people are tied to that identity more deeply than others. Some of you may have already started letting pieces of it go, while others still feel like that version of yourself is the only version that ever fully made sense. Wherever you fall in that, it doesn't make you right or wrong. It just means that part of your life mattered to you in a way that left a mark, and when something shapes you that deeply, it stays with you long after the environment itself is gone.

It's okay to miss that person. It's okay to miss the way you felt when things were clear, when your role made sense, and when the structure around you gave you a kind of confidence and certainty that didn't need to be questioned. Missing that doesn't mean you're failing to move forward, and it doesn't mean you're stuck in the past. It means you experienced something that shaped you deeply enough to leave an imprint that doesn't simply disappear because time passed. Honestly, you'd be a fool not to miss it, because that part of your life carried something most people will never fully understand. It gave you a sense of purpose, connection, and meaning that wasn't surface level. It wasn't casual, and it wasn't built under normal circumstances. It was built under pressure, in environments where people relied on each other completely and where what you did actually mattered in immediate and visible ways.

That kind of connection doesn't just disappear. There's a saying we use—miss the monkeys, not the circus—and that's exactly what a lot of this becomes over time. You don't always miss the system. You don't always miss every part of the organization or everything that came with it. But you miss the people. You miss the ones you served with, the ones who understood you without needing things explained, and the ones who existed beside you during experiences that most people outside that world will never fully relate to. Relationships built in those environments carry a different kind of weight because they were formed under pressure, where trust wasn't theoretical and where people saw sides of each other that rarely come out anywhere else. There's a depth to those connections that normal life doesn't always recreate easily, and losing regular access to that kind of bond can leave a space in you that takes a long time to fully understand.

For some people, there's something even heavier underneath all of that: the people who didn't make it. The ones who don't get to figure this part out. The ones who don't get to move forward, even when moving forward feels confusing or painful. The ones whose stories stopped while yours kept going. When you sit with that long enough, it can turn into guilt. You start asking questions that don't have answers. Why them? Why not me? And if you hold onto those questions the wrong way, they can keep you trapped in something that never fully resolves. You can spend years replaying it in your head, trying to make sense of something that simply doesn't make sense in a way that feels fair.

I've had to learn that there are some questions in life that don't give you closure. But I've also learned there's another way to carry those memories. Because what you had with those people—what you saw, what you experienced together, the way you knew them—is something most of the world will never fully understand. You got to see people stripped down to who they really were underneath everything else. You saw courage, fear, sacrifice, humor, loyalty, and humanity in environments where none of it could be faked for very long. Those experiences don't disappear once the environment is gone. They become part of you in ways that continue shaping how you see the world long after those moments are over.

That's the part you don't lose. Not the title or the role, but the people, the lessons, and the perspective that came with those experiences. Over time, I've started understanding that carrying those things forward doesn't mean staying trapped in the past. It means allowing those experiences to continue shaping who you are without letting them prevent you from becoming something more than only that version of yourself. This isn't about forgetting where you came from. It's about learning how to carry it in a way that strengthens you instead of holding you down. You don't move on from it. You carry it forward.

Mission Debrief – Carrying It

1. What are you trying to hide—and what might change if you stopped hiding it?
2. Are you carrying your experiences as something to suppress... or something to understand?
3. What would it look like for you to give your experiences purpose instead of just holding onto them?
4. Who are you choosing to be now—and how is that influenced by the people you served with?
5. What part of your story could help someone else feel less alone if you were willing to share it?

20

The Brand New Old You

When You Start to Recognize Yourself Again

This part doesn't happen fast. There isn't a moment where everything suddenly clicks back into place or where you wake up one day and feel completely like yourself again. It's slower than that. It takes time, and it takes deliberate effort in ways that don't always feel significant while they're happening. Some days feel steady, like you're finally moving in the right direction and beginning to gain ground again. Other days feel heavier, like you've slid backward and everything you've been working toward isn't holding together the way you hoped it would.

It's an uneven process, and it doesn't look the same for everyone. Some people move through it in smaller waves—periods of adjustment they can work through without losing too much footing. Others hit deeper points, places that feel harder to climb out of, where the progress doesn't feel visible and the effort itself starts to feel exhausting. But even though the details are different, there's usually something underneath it that connects people going through this kind of transition. There's common ground in the experience of trying to rebuild yourself after parts of your identity, structure, or purpose no longer feel as solid as they once did.

That's where connection starts to matter in a different way. Because when you reach a point where you don't fully trust what you see in yourself anymore, it helps to have people around you who remember you clearly. The people who knew you before everything became complicated. The people who remember how you carried yourself, how you showed up, and what you were capable of long before you started questioning all of it yourself. Not because they can pull you backward into who you used to be, but because they can remind you that the good parts of you didn't disappear just because you lost sight of them for a while.

Sometimes that's what grounding actually looks like. It's not someone fixing things for you, and it's not someone pretending everything is okay when it isn't. It's someone helping you reconnect with parts of yourself you stopped recognizing. Someone reflecting back pieces of you that became harder to see clearly while you were buried underneath everything else. When you've spent long enough questioning your own value, your own identity, or your own direction, that kind of reminder matters more than people realize.

Over time, those moments start making a difference. Slowly, you begin recognizing small pieces of yourself again. Not all at once, and not in a way that feels complete or dramatic, but enough to notice. You start seeing it in the way you respond under pressure, in the way you handle situations that once would have pulled you apart, and in the way you show up for the people around you when it actually matters. Those moments seem small from the outside, but internally they carry weight because they remind you that not everything inside you disappeared.

It's not the same as it was before, and honestly, it's not supposed to be. You've been through too much for everything to simply reset back to what it once was. But that doesn't mean there's nothing left to build from. It means you're learning how to recognize yourself in a different form. Not as the exact person you used to be, but as someone who still carries those same core pieces underneath everything you've experienced since then.

And that realization starts to matter more over time because it shows you that you're not rebuilding from nothing. Even after everything that changed, there are still parts of you worth holding onto. There are still values, strengths, and pieces of your identity that survived even when other things fell apart. You're not creating yourself out of empty space. You're rebuilding from something that was still there all along, even when you couldn't fully see it yet.

Mission Debrief – Recognizing Yourself

1. Where in your life do you still see pieces of the person you used to be?
2. Who in your life has seen you at your best—and can help remind you of that?
3. Are you expecting yourself to feel "fully back"... or are you recognizing progress in smaller moments?
4. When things feel off, who can help ground you in what's real instead of what you're telling yourself?
5. What would change if you trusted that parts of you are still there—even if they don't feel accessible right now?

21

Reaching Back

Being the Support You Needed

I didn't write this because I have all the answers. I wrote it because I didn't want someone else walking into this blind the way I did. Not because I can protect anyone from all of it—that's not possible. There's no version of transition where you avoid every difficult part of it, where you move through it without feeling the confusion, the loss, the anger, or the weight that comes with trying to rebuild yourself after everything changes. Some of that is simply part of the experience.

But you don't have to face it alone.

If anything, I think of this less as a guide and more as a set of caution signs. Not something that tells you exactly where to go or guarantees you won't struggle, but something that helps you recognize what's happening while you're inside it. Something that gives you a chance to slow down long enough to understand what you're carrying before it completely takes over your life. Because that's where a lot of us get caught. We don't recognize what's happening while it's unfolding. We just react to it. We push through it, avoid it, bury it, or try to outwork it until eventually we look back and realize we've already gone farther into it than we ever intended to.

That's what I'm trying to change.

Not by pretending I have some perfect roadmap, and not by telling anyone exactly how they should live their life, but by being honest about what it looked like for me. The mistakes, the avoidance, the anger, the confusion, and the parts I didn't understand until much later. Because I believe there's a reason I went through what I did. Not in a way that magically makes everything okay, and not in a way that excuses the damage that happened along the way, but in a way that gives the experience meaning beyond just my own suffering.

I believe part of the reason I survived it was so I could reach back.

So I could help someone else recognize the signs sooner. So maybe someone else doesn't have to lose as much of themselves before they finally understand what's happening. So maybe someone else reads this and realizes they aren't weak, broken beyond repair, or completely alone in what they're experiencing. Sometimes that kind of realization matters more than advice ever could.

Because that's what we've always done.

We reach back for each other.

Even before any of this, that was part of the culture we carried with us. You take care of your people. You become someone others can rely on. You show up when it matters—not only for yourself, but for the people standing beside you. That mindset doesn't disappear just because the uniform comes off. The environment changes, but the responsibility to look out for each other doesn't suddenly stop existing.

It just starts showing up in different ways.

Now the opportunity looks different than it used to. It may not happen in a combat zone, inside a unit, or during the kinds of moments that once defined your life. Instead, it shows up in conversations, in honesty, in recognizing when someone is struggling before they know how to say it themselves. It shows up in being the person who understands what someone means when they say they feel lost, angry, disconnected, or unsure of who they are anymore.

That matters more than most people realize.

Because for someone else, that conversation might be the first time they feel understood in a long time. It might be the first time someone recognizes what they're carrying without forcing them to explain every piece of it. Sometimes the biggest shift doesn't come from some life-changing speech or dramatic moment. Sometimes it comes from realizing another person truly understands what it feels like to sit in that space.

That's how this carries forward.

Not by fixing everything for each other, because none of us can do that. Some parts of this are still difficult no matter how much support you have. But we can make sure people don't have to carry it completely alone. We can make sure someone else knows there's still a way forward even when they can't fully see it yet.

A lot of the time, that starts with something simple.

Just showing up.

That's all this book is really meant to be. Not a perfect answer, not a checklist, and not a solution to every part of transition. Just one person reaching back for the people coming behind him and saying, "I know what this feels like, and you're not the only one trying to figure it out."

Sometimes a small piece of help along the way is enough to change where someone ends up.

Mission Debrief – Reaching Back

1. Who in your life could benefit from you showing up—not as someone who has answers, but as someone who understands?
2. What experiences have you been through that could help someone else feel less alone?
3. Are you waiting until you feel "fully put together" to help others—or can you show up as you are now?
4. What would it look like for you to "reach back" in your own way?
5. How can you become someone others can count on—without losing yourself in the process?

22

Being More Than A Tool

A Means to an End

That phrase gets a bad reputation. “A means to an end” sounds like something disposable—like you don’t matter, like you’re only valuable for what you can provide to someone else. It makes it seem like there’s no worth in who you are as a person, only in how useful you can be. I understand why people push back against it, because when it’s viewed that way, it strips away identity and reduces people down to tools instead of human beings.

But that’s never been how I’ve understood it.

I don’t see it as losing value. I see it as creating it. Because being a means to an end doesn’t mean you don’t matter—it means you can become part of something bigger than yourself in a way that actually changes another person’s life. It means you can be the moment that helps someone hold on a little longer. You can be the conversation that shifts something in someone who felt completely stuck. You can be the person whose honesty makes someone else realize they aren’t alone, even if they haven’t spoken a word out loud about what they’re carrying.

That’s not being used.

That’s choosing to show up.

And there's a difference between those two things that matters more than people realize. One takes your humanity away. The other is an intentional act of connection. It's choosing to let what you've lived through become something that reaches beyond just your own pain. It's allowing your experience to create value for someone else instead of letting it exist only as something that hurt you.

That changed the way I started looking at everything I went through.

For a long time, I only saw my experiences through the lens of what they cost me. The things I lost. The mistakes I made. The relationships I strained. The parts of myself I didn't recognize anymore. But eventually I started understanding that if I was willing to be honest about those things, then maybe they could serve a purpose beyond just my own suffering. Maybe they could help someone else recognize what was happening to them before they lost as much of themselves as I did.

Sometimes that kind of connection matters more than advice ever could.

Because when someone is truly struggling, they're not always looking for perfect answers. Most of the time they're looking for proof that another person has sat in that same darkness and found some way to keep moving through it. They're looking for something real enough to hold onto when everything in their own head is telling them to let go.

And sometimes that's enough.

Sometimes all it takes is one moment, one conversation, or one realization that things do not have to stay exactly the way they feel right now. Sometimes hearing another person say, "I know what that feels like," carries more weight than people understand because it interrupts the isolation that keeps so many people trapped inside themselves.

If I can be part of that for someone else, then what I went through carries meaning beyond just my own experience.

And the same can be true for you.

You don't need to have everything figured out before you can show up for someone else. You don't need to be perfectly healed, perfectly stable, or completely at peace with your own life before you can make a difference in another person's. Most of the time, what actually matters is your willingness to be honest, present, and real enough for someone else to feel safe being honest too.

That's where connection starts.

Not in perfection, but in honesty.

Because when someone is sitting in that place—when things feel heavy, when life stops making sense, and when they don't know if they still have the energy to keep fighting—they usually aren't looking for someone with a flawless answer. They're looking for a reason to stay. A reason to believe there's still something ahead of them worth reaching for, even if they can't fully see it yet.

Sometimes another human being becomes that reason.

Sometimes simply knowing they aren't alone anymore changes everything.

And if what I've lived through allows me to be part of that for someone else, then none of it was meaningless.

Mission Debrief – A Means to an End

1. What does "being a means to an end" mean to you—and is it something you've rejected without redefining?
2. How could your presence or your story help someone else keep going, even for a moment?
3. Are you waiting until you feel "worthy" to make an impact—or can you do that as you are now?
4. What would it look like for you to show up in a way that benefits someone else, without losing yourself in the process?
5. Who might need you to simply be there—not to fix anything, but to remind them they're not alone?

23

Guidance In the Silence

When It Gets Quiet

No one prepares you for the quiet. Not the kind of quiet that feels peaceful, where you finally get to rest after everything you've been through. Not the kind that brings relief or gives you a sense that the hard part is finally over. This is a different kind of quiet entirely. It's the kind that shows up after everything stops moving. After the chaos settles, after the structure disappears, and after the mission ends without anything immediately replacing it. It doesn't hit all at once either. It settles in slowly, almost quietly at first, until one day you realize it's there and somehow feels heavier than everything that came before it.

There's a moment where life is supposed to feel normal again. You're home. You're safe. You're out. People expect that to mean something. They expect relief, happiness, or some kind of visible peace after everything you've experienced. And part of you tries to match that expectation. You try to feel what everyone assumes you're supposed to feel now that the difficult part is technically over. But internally, nothing lines up the way you thought it would. Everything that once gave your life direction and certainty is suddenly gone. There's no formation, no mission, no immediate responsibility demanding your attention. There's no clear definition of what "right" even looks like anymore. There's just space, time, and a mind that doesn't seem to know how to slow down.

That's when the quiet starts getting loud. Because once everything external falls away, you're left alone with yourself. All the things you didn't have time to process, all the thoughts you pushed down just to get through the day, and all the moments that never fully made sense at the time don't disappear simply because the environment changed. They wait. And when life finally slows down enough, they come back all at once. Not in order, not in a way that feels manageable, and not in a form that's easy to explain to anyone else. Just fragments of everything you've carried surfacing at the same time without any clear system for how to deal with them.

No one really hands you a blueprint for that part. There's no checklist for how to sit alone with your own thoughts after years of surviving inside structure, urgency, and constant movement. Most conversations around transition focus on practical things—getting out, finding work, building a new routine, or creating stability again. Those things matter, but this is the part that often catches people off guard. This is where a lot of people actually get lost, not in the middle of chaos, but in the absence of it.

Because chaos at least gives you direction. It tells you where to go, what matters, and what needs to happen next. The quiet doesn't give you any of that. Instead, it asks questions you may not be prepared to answer. Who are you now? What are you supposed to build your life around? What matters when everything that once defined you no longer exists in the same form? If you don't have something solid to anchor yourself to, it becomes very easy to start drifting without even realizing it.

I wish I could say there was some defining moment where everything suddenly clicked for me, where I figured it all out and life immediately started making sense again. That's not what happened. There wasn't some dramatic breakthrough or realization that instantly changed everything. What actually happened was much smaller than that. Almost unnoticeable at first. It was just a series of decisions that didn't feel important in the moment but slowly became the reason I kept moving forward instead of completely shutting down.

Getting out of bed on days where I didn't really see a reason to. Showing up for my family even when I didn't feel like I deserved to be there. Doing something physical, anything at all, just to get out of my own head for a little while. Not because I felt motivated or inspired, and not because I suddenly discovered some larger sense of purpose that made everything easier, but because I didn't trust what would happen if I stopped trying entirely. At the time, that didn't feel like progress. It just felt like survival. But looking back now, those small decisions mattered more than I understood then.

One of the hardest things for me to accept was that progress wasn't going to look the way I thought it would. It wasn't going to arrive through achievements, recognition, or some obvious sign that I had "made it" to the other side of transition. Most of the time it looked much quieter than that. It looked like staying. It looked like choosing not to disappear on the days where disappearing would have felt easier. It looked like learning how to sit with things I didn't fully understand without immediately trying to escape them. It looked like accepting that I wasn't going to become the exact same person I was before and learning how to continue living anyway.

The truth is, the quiet never completely goes away. It still shows up, just in different ways and at different times. Some days it feels manageable. Other days it doesn't. But over time, something begins to shift in the way you relate to it. It stops feeling like something constantly trying to drag you under and starts becoming something you can sit beside without immediately feeling consumed by it. Not comfortably, and not in a way that suddenly makes everything easy, but in a way that no longer terrifies you the way it once did.

If you're sitting in that space right now, where things aren't actively falling apart but they also aren't fully coming together, where you're not necessarily in crisis but you also know you're not okay, then this is that part. This is the quiet. And if all you're doing right now is getting through the day, that matters more than you probably realize. Because sometimes the mission isn't fixing everything or finally figuring your entire life out. Sometimes the mission is simply staying. Staying long enough for things to slowly begin shifting underneath the surface, even when you can't fully see it yet.

There's no moment where the quiet suddenly makes perfect sense. There's no clean transition into peace or certainty. Most of the time it's just time, effort, repetition, and the decision to keep being here again and again, even when it doesn't feel like any of it is leading anywhere. Somehow, though, you keep going. And eventually, without realizing exactly when it happened, you start understanding that continuing to move forward—even slowly—is its own kind of victory.

24

For the 22

Still in It

There is no perfect ending. But then again, we were never in this for perfect. From the beginning, nothing about this was clean. Nothing followed a straight path, and nothing resolved itself in a way that suddenly made everything make sense. That's not what this journey is, and honestly, it never was. What a lot of us learned—whether we wanted to or not—is that happiness doesn't just appear once all the hard parts are over. It isn't waiting at the finish line for us after everything finally settles down. Most of the time, it's something we build slowly, piece by piece, in the middle of the mess while we're still carrying parts of everything we've been through.

The road doesn't suddenly smooth out either. It doesn't become perfectly clear, and there usually isn't a moment where you feel fully "arrived." What changes instead is the way you move through it. You learn how to carry things differently. You learn how to keep walking even when parts of the path still feel uncertain underneath you. I remember sitting in moments where everything felt like it had stopped moving. Not in a peaceful way, but in a way where nothing made sense anymore. The noise was gone, but so was the direction. I wasn't actively fighting anymore, but I also didn't feel like I was truly living either. I was existing somewhere in between who I had been and whatever I was supposed to become next. That in-between space is where a lot of people get stuck, because no one really tells you what to do once the mission ends but your life keeps going.

That part is heavier than most people realize. We've lost too many people in that space. Good people. Strong people. Capable people who had years of experience, families who loved them, and entire futures still sitting in front of them, but who couldn't find a way to reconnect to life after everything they had already given away. People who stopped seeing a version of the future that felt meaningful enough to keep moving toward. People who carried things silently because they didn't know how to explain what was happening inside them, or because they thought they were supposed to be able to handle it on their own.

People talk about "22 a day," but most of us know the reality is more complicated than a number people repeat online. We know there are more stories than most people are comfortable sitting with, and more pain than most conversations are willing to hold. When you've seen enough of it up close, you stop looking at it like a statistic and start understanding it for what it really is: people who lost connection to themselves, to purpose, or to the belief that things could still become something different than what they were feeling in that moment.

That's the truth of it. This doesn't end cleanly. There isn't a moment where everything suddenly clicks into place and you wake up completely okay. There isn't some perfect resolution where every difficult thought disappears and every wound finally closes. What there is instead is movement. Sometimes small movement. Sometimes movement so quiet you barely recognize it while it's happening. Days where getting out of bed is the victory. Days where you don't feel like yourself but still choose to keep going anyway. Days where nothing outwardly changes, but internally you're still fighting to stay present instead of disappearing into yourself again.

And honestly, those days matter more than people realize. Because we don't get perfect endings. What we get is the opportunity to keep moving forward. We get the chance to carry what we've been through without allowing it to become the only thing that defines who we are. We get the opportunity to accept that we are different now—not ruined, not beyond repair, but changed in ways we never asked for and never fully expected. Maybe that's where healing actually begins. Not when everything is fixed, but when we stop waiting for perfection before allowing ourselves to keep living.

There is no clean resolution waiting for us at the end of all this. There is only truth. There is only forward movement. There is only the decision to stay here long enough to continue becoming something more than the worst moments we've lived through. Maybe that's what returning to being actually looks like—not becoming who you were before, not erasing what happened, but learning how to carry all of it while still allowing yourself to move forward anyway. Some way, somehow, to return to being.

Afterward

What you just read isn't a guide. It's not a checklist, and it's not something you follow step by step and suddenly come out the other side with everything figured out. That's not how this works. It never did, at least not in anything I went through. There wasn't a clean path, there wasn't a moment where everything lined up perfectly, and there wasn't a single answer I could point to and say this is what fixed everything. Most of the time, it didn't even feel like progress while it was happening. It just felt like surviving one day at a time and trying to make decisions that kept me moving instead of falling further backward.

What this is instead is proof. Not the kind of proof that comes with perfect answers or guarantees, but the kind that shows you something is still possible even when it doesn't feel like it. Proof that you can lose yourself in a way that feels complete, in a way that makes it hard to recognize anything that once felt familiar, and still find something inside you that allows you to keep moving forward. Not all at once, and not in a way that suddenly makes life make sense again, but enough to keep going long enough for things to slowly begin changing underneath the surface.

There were moments in my life where I genuinely didn't think I was going to make it through. Not because I wanted everything to end, and not because I had fully given up on life, but because I didn't know how to exist in a world that no longer felt the way it used to. The structure that held everything together was gone. The purpose that once felt clear didn't feel the same anymore. The identity I had built myself around no longer fit in the way I understood it before, and I didn't know what was supposed to replace it once it was gone.

That's a difficult place to sit in because it's quiet in a way that's hard to explain and heavy in a way that doesn't always show up on the outside.

Most people around you may not even realize how much you're carrying because a lot of this happens internally. It lives in the thoughts you don't know how to explain, the distance you feel from yourself, and the exhaustion that comes from trying to hold everything together while quietly wondering why none of it feels right anymore. When you stay in that space long enough, it starts to feel permanent. It starts to feel like maybe this is just what life is now, and maybe this version of you is all that's left.

If you're sitting in that place right now, I want you to hear this in a way that doesn't sound rehearsed or forced. You are not done. Not because everything is suddenly going to become easy, and not because someone is going to appear and fix all of it for you. Life doesn't work that way. But because there is still something inside you that hasn't disappeared, even if you can't fully feel it yet. There is still a part of you responding underneath all the exhaustion, confusion, anger, or numbness. There is still something in you capable of movement, even if right now that movement feels slow and almost impossible to recognize.

That part matters more than you think it does.

This book exists because I made it through that space. Not perfectly, and not in a way I would ever try to present as clean or controlled. There were setbacks. There were moments where it felt like nothing was changing at all. There were days where I questioned whether any of the effort I was putting in actually mattered. But I stayed long enough to eventually realize that something underneath all of it was shifting, even when I couldn't immediately see it happening myself.

Eventually, that became enough to turn around and start reaching back for other people.

Not because I suddenly became someone with all the answers, but because I knew what it felt like to sit in that place and honestly believe there wasn't a way out of it. Everything I'm doing now—whether it's speaking openly about this, writing, building things for other veterans, or simply being honest about what transition can actually feel like—comes from that same place. Not from certainty, but from understanding what it feels like to live without it. Because no one should have to carry this completely alone.

If there's anything to take from this, it isn't some grand lesson or formula. It's something much simpler than that. You do not need to have everything figured out right now. You do not need to feel fully healed. You do not need to become the exact person you were before everything changed, because that version of you may not exist in the same way anymore. And honestly, that's okay. What matters is that you keep moving. Even if the movement is slow. Even if it doesn't fully make sense yet. Even if all you can do right now is make one decision that keeps you from falling back into the place you fought so hard to survive.

That still counts.

Probably more than you give yourself credit for.

And if you're still here—still reading this, still trying to figure out what comes next, still carrying whatever it is you've been carrying—then you are already doing more than you think you are. It might not feel like progress yet, and it might not look like anything significant from the outside, but it matters. Sometimes surviving long enough to continue searching for a way forward is progress, even when it doesn't feel meaningful in the moment.

We're all still in it in one way or another. All of us are carrying different experiences, different losses, different questions, and different versions of ourselves that we're still trying to understand. None of this lines up perfectly the way we imagined it would, and most of the time there isn't a clean answer waiting for us at the end of it all. But somehow, even in the middle of all that uncertainty, people still keep finding ways to move forward.

And maybe that's enough.

Maybe that's where hope actually begins.